BEYOND BEDLAM

KEN SMITH is the author of many poetry collections including *The Poet Reclining* (1982, revised edition 1989), *Wormwood* (1987) and *Tender to the Queen of Spain* (1993), and two books of non-fiction, *Inside Time* (1989) and *Berlin: Coming in from the Cold* (1990).

MATTHEW SWEENEY has published seven collections of poetry including two for children. He co-edited the anthology *Emergency Kit* (1996) with Jo Shapcott, and co-wrote *Writing Poetry* (1997) with John Hartley Williams. His latest collection of poetry for adults is *The Bridal Suite* (1997).

Sketch to illustrate the Passions.
Agony – Raving Madness, 1854.
Richard Dadd (1817–86)

Sketch of an idea for Crazy Jane, 1855. Richard Dadd (1817–86)

Beyond Bedlam

POEMS WRITTEN OUT OF MENTAL DISTRESS

Edited by Ken Smith & Matthew Sweeney

With a Foreword by Dr Felix Post

ANVIL PRESS POETRY

First published 1997 by Anvil Press Poetry Ltd
Neptune House 70 Royal Hill London SE10 8RT

First impression

This book is published with financial assistance from
The Arts Council of England

Designed and typeset by Anvil in Monotype Janson
Printed and bound in England by
Cromwell Press, Melksham, Wiltshire

ISBN 0 85646 296 9

A Solitary Child, c. 1967.
Marion Patrick (1940–93)

This longing to commit a madness stays with us throughout our lives. Who has not, when standing with someone by an abyss or high up on a tower, had a sudden impulse to push the other over. And how is it that we hurt those we love although we know that remorse will follow... Our whole being is nothing but a fight against the dark forces within ourselves.

HENRIK IBSEN

Poetry, thank God, remained within my grasp, and, having always loved it, I now fell upon it with a passion that is hard to describe.

KAY REDFIELD JAMISON: *An Unquiet Mind*

The Cross, c. 1967.
Marion Patrick

Lord Clark of Saltwood, 1977.
Stanley Lench (b. 1934)

CONTENTS

It Has Not Worked, 1974.
Charlotte Johnson

Foreword

Since my retirement from the Bethlem Royal Hospital and the Maudsley Hospital in 1978 I have been working through some 400 biographies of famous men, all of whom had died during the last 150 years.* Like other recent investigators I found, against popular belief, that 'geniuses' had fallen victim of insanity rather less frequently than ordinary people. However, serious disorders of personality were more common in artists and creative writers, while emotional breakdowns, mainly depressive illnesses, had afflicted creative writers twice as often as visual artists, composers, thinkers, national leaders and scientists, all of whom had suffered depressive breakdowns to a similar extent as members of the general population. (A high level of depressive disorders has also been found in living writers by other recent workers.) The writers and artists differed, however, from ordinary people not only on account of their high general ability and special gifts, but also equally strikingly in terms of their painstaking industriousness, perseverance, and toughness in the face of adversity and hardship caused by initial neglect of, or hostility towards, their creative achievements.

To my great surprise, and in contradiction of long accepted and recently restated opinions to the effect that, as Lord Byron claimed, all poets were mad, I found that writers who had published only poetry had suffered less often from depressions, alcoholism, social and sexual maladjustments than those who had also or only produced prose fiction or plays.† This was the case inspite of the fact that the great majority of all kinds of writers were equally predisposed to depressive breakdowns by their hypersensitive and emotionally vulnerable personalities.

---

* It was not my intention to concentrate solely on men, but in all my reading I had only been able to find sufficiently complete biographies of one female scientist and of five women writers, and this small number had to be omitted from my analysis.

† Felix Post, 'Verbal Creativity, Depression and Alcoholism: An Investigation of One Hundred American and British Writers', *British Journal of Psychiatry* (1996), 168, pp. 545–55.

they have avoided depression or even madness, and my findings suggest that the self-therapy of writing poetry may be more effective than the writing of novels or plays. Putting into harmonious and rhythmical language one's own inner sufferings and distress in the concentrated form of a lyric poem might be more therapeutic than empathizing at length with the trials and tribulations of the imagined characters of one's novels or plays, an activity which may indeed aggravate depressive tendencies.

The investigation continues, but my current suggestion is that writing poetry may well be helpful in achieving recovery from depressive illnesses and the avoidance of their recurrence. However, very special gifts and hard work at achieving the craft of writing poetry are needed to create out of mental distress poems of the quality presented in this volume.

FELIX POST
London, July 1997

Bedlam and Beyond

This book developed from a project originating with a group at the Maudsley who were inspired by the quantity and quality of poetry being produced by patients, or 'users', of the Bethlem & Maudsley hospitals. Creative work produced in this way is rarely considered in its own right and tends to be dismissed as 'merely therapy', an example of the stigma which surrounds mental illness. In giving a voice to this work we hope to challenge this assumption.

The 750th Anniversary of the founding of the Royal Bethlem Hospital – the original 'Bedlam' – provided an ideal occasion for commemoration in a book. With the initial aim of publishing some of this material for the occasion, we convened as a voluntary group, with a range of backgrounds in psychiatry, psychology, marketing and publishing, and also direct experience as poets and patients. When Ken Smith and Matthew Sweeney joined us as editors, the book's scope was widened to place some of this and other work gathered from similar sources side by side with the work of recognized poets, past and present.

The response to our public appeal for material was amazing. Work poured in from all parts of the UK and Ireland after word of the project went out through the mental health community, poetry magazines and the networks of Survivors' Poetry, an innovative national organization dedicated to promoting the poetry and self-empowerment of users and survivors. Most of the 5,000-odd submissions came from previously unpublished authors. The quality of work received was impressive and much of it deeply moving; one of the hardest things about the project was the realization that much valuable work would be left unpublished.

In the course of the project's development issues of quality, focus and purpose were much debated. What unified and sustained the project was an interest shared among ourselves and with our partners in some of the conceptual issues at stake. What role can poetry have in alleviating symptoms of mental distress; how is it used; what does it reveal; and what evidence is there of a real exchange between creativity and 'madness'?

The subject itself has been tackled from many angles before us.

It is a decidedly rich one, historically, philosophically, artistically and clinically; from the Renaissance fool to Surrealism, from Byron to Berryman, and from Freud to Foucault. 'Madness' has been both held to reveal inner truth and condemned to silence and exclusion as something unintelligible by reason, and therefore threatening to society and to humanity. It is clear that creative expression can help in the understanding and handling of intense emotional states, and that reading and writing poetry can serve a therapeutic function by articulating and transforming the inner world. As poetry enables the communication of experiences beyond the constraints of everyday language, so the dialogue between extremes of language and emotional experience can produce something new and precious.

This project has received tremendous support from every quarter we turned to for help: from the initial response to the idea within the mental health community to the support of the Bethlem & Maudsley Trust, and in particular a group collecting poems from staff and patients within the joint hospitals, with whom we were able to collaborate as complementary national and local projects; from the charities nominated by workers in the mental health sector throughout Britain and Ireland to benefit from the project – MIND, the Mental Health Foundation and Survivors' Poetry – to the Poetry Society and the Arts Council; and finally from the enthusiasm of the editors to the commitment of Anvil Press. In particular, we would like to thank Judith Beare, David Stedman, Patricia Allderidge, Liz Aram, Charlotte Munday, Jean Dixon, Alison Combes, Judy Gascoyne and Felix Post, and of course the writers whose poems originally inspired us and without whose contributions this book could not exist.

DANIEL BROWN
Psychologist, Institute of Psychiatry

RICHARD HALLWARD
National Projects Manager, Investors in People UK

SARAH HASAN MAJID
Registrar in Psychotherapy, Bethlem & Maudsley Trust

RAVI WICKREMASINGHE
Publishing Manager, Barnardo's

CHARLOTTE WILSON JONES
Registrar in Psychiatry, Bethlem & Maudsley Trust

THE BETHLEM & MAUDSLEY TRUST 750th ANNIVERSARY
NATIONAL BENEFIT POETRY PROJECT COMMITTEE

Introduction

It is the unconscious that drives poetry, the jumps and sudden lurches that forge new connections with things not connected before, new ways of seeing. And it is also in the unconscious that the voices of the irrational lurk. Perhaps this is why, according to a study by Kay Redfield Jamison, poets are thirty times more likely to undergo a depressive illness than the rest of the population, and twenty times more likely to be committed to an asylum.*

In recent years much has been made of the uses of creative writing as therapy. The results do not always settle well as poetry, however valuable they may be as treatment or expression. Much of the material that we read in the course of compiling this book – more than five thousand poems had been submitted to the Maudsley group who commissioned us to edit it – was raw experience, untransmuted. Some of this was difficult to cope with, to absorb emotionally; the experiences behind it were all too real and the cumulative effect often depressing. From time to time, however, we came across pieces that rose beyond their immediate occasion – that transmuted the original experience into art.

These were the poems which gave this anthology its purpose. The perspective was soon broadened by our interest in many relevant poems by recent and contemporary writers; and the anthologies published by Survivors' Poetry gave us further sources. But poems written out of mental distress are not just a contemporary phenomenon. For historical perspective we went to the canon of existing work, to poems which have sprung from such disturbances or which address aspects of the subject by poets like Christopher Smart, John Clare, Anne Sexton, Robert Lowell, Sylvia Plath. This strategy provided continuity and a context in which to set unknown contemporaries in suffering, so that lesser known or previously unpublished writers rub shoulders with famous names. This mix and the sense of a continuum are to our minds among the book's most exciting features.

---

* Reported in the *Independent on Sunday*, 29 June 1997.

A surprise for some readers might be the range of moods to be found in these pages – humour as well as gloom, beauty as well as despair, calm as well as chaos. The poems show that mental disorder, rather than being a condition suffered by a few, can approach and invade very many lives – 'people like us', as Peter Reading says. And the fact was that both of us had had brushes with mental instability, and had come to see how vital our own writing was in helping us deal with it, how the act of writing can help offset the advance of chaos, shaping it into the order of words. It was perhaps this that drew us to the project in the first place when we were approached, separately, as possible editors: and which made us want to undertake it jointly.

This therapeutic property of writing was as evident in many of the poems we didn't include as in those we did. In the end, rather than settling for a random or alphabetical order, we shaped our selected text as an implicit narrative: beginning with the fear of madness, its foreshadowing, its sudden or its slow coming on, then the long throes of it, the dealing with it afterwards, perhaps long afterwards – the living with it. For those who visit that wild country and return, normality can never be the same again.

KEN SMITH & MATTHEW SWEENEY

Me, Myself, I, 1987.
Allan Beveridge (b. 1946)

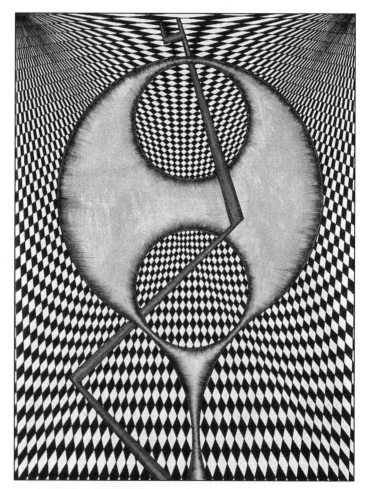

Thought, 1986. David Chick (b. 1947)

Beyond Bedlam

The first Day's Night had come…

The first Day's Night had come –
And grateful that a thing
So terrible – had been endured –
I told my Soul to sing –

She said her Strings were snapt –
Her Bow – to Atoms blown –
And so to mend her – gave me work
Until another Morn –

And then – a Day as huge
As Yesterdays in pairs,
Unrolled its horror in my face –
Until it blocked my eyes –

My Brain – begun to laugh –
I mumbled – like a fool –
And tho' 'tis Years ago – that Day –
My Brain keeps giggling – still.

And Something's odd – within –
That person that I was –
And this One – do not feel the same –
Could it be Madness – this?

EMILY DICKINSON (1830–86)

Apprehensions

There is this white wall, above which the sky creates itself –
Infinite, green, utterly untouchable.
Angels swim in it, and the stars, in indifference also.
They are my medium.
The sun dissolves on this wall, bleeding its lights.

A grey wall now, clawed and bloody.
Is there no way out of the mind?
Steps at my back spiral into a well.
There are no trees or birds in this world,
There is only a sourness.

This red wall winces continually:
A red fist, opening and closing,
Two grey, papery bags –
This is what I am made of, this, and a terror
Of being wheeled off under crosses and a rain of pieties.

On a black wall, unidentifiable birds
Swivel their heads and cry.
There is no talk of immortality among these!
Cold blanks approach us:
They move in a hurry.

SYLVIA PLATH (1932–63)

from
Grace Abounding to the Chief of Sinners

Thus was I always sinking, whatever I did think or do. So one day I walked to a neighbouring town, and sat down upon a settle in the street, and fell into a very deep pause about the most fearful state my sin had brought me to; and, after long musing, I lifted up my head, but methought I saw as if the sun that shineth in the heavens did grudge to give light, and as if the very stones in the street, and tiles upon the houses, did bend themselves against me; methought that they all combined together to banish me out of the world; I was abhorred of them, and unfit to dwell among them, or be partaker of their benefits, because I had sinned against the Saviour. O how happy, now, was every creature over what I was; for they stood fast and kept their station, but I was gone and lost.

JOHN BUNYAN (1628–88)

I Know I'm a Sick Man

I know I'm a sick man. I know
That in me who I am is missing.
Yes, but, as long as I'm not submitting,
I'd like to know the way I'm going.

Though I go towards submitting me
To the thing Destiny makes me be,
I *would* like, one moment, to stop
Here   and at my ease take stock.

There's great lapses of memory,
Great parallel lost lines
And a lot of legend and a lot of history
And lots of lives, lots of lives –

All that; from me now I am losing
Me, astray's where I go – I'd call
Out to me, and am enclosing
My self within recalling all.

I'd like, if it's mad I'm going to be,
To be mad sagely and morally.
I'm going, like Nero, to strum the lyre.
Only there's no need for the fire.

FERNANDO PESSOA (1888–1935)
Translated by Jonathan Griffin

Hysteria

As she laughed I was aware of becoming involved in her laughter and being part of it, until her teeth were only accidental stars with a talent for squad-drill. I was drawn in by short gasps, inhaled at each momentary recovery, lost finally in the dark caverns of her throat, bruised by the ripple of unseen muscles. An elderly waiter with trembling hands was hurriedly spreading a pink and white checked cloth over the rusty green iron table, saying: 'If the lady and gentleman wish to take their tea in the garden, if the lady and gentleman wish to take their tea in the garden...' I decided that if the shaking of her breasts could be stopped, some of the fragments of the afternoon might be collected, and I concentrated my attention with careful subtlety to this end.

T.S. ELIOT (1886–1965)

Uncoupling

Halfway
home, she
feels the
first
flicker of
fear from
midriff
to throat.

So she
flicks the
switch
in her
head to
dis-
connect
her face.

EAMER O'KEEFFE (*b.* 1940)

Out of Order

Eyes not seeing too well
The right things.
Ears not hearing too well
What my soul, unanswered, begs for.

SOLOMON BLUE WATERS

The Hole

Uncertain, unsteadily,
I walked down the familiar path.
Sparrows cried out warnings to me:
'There's a hole ahead'
I ignored them, as usual,
Thinking 'It's only delusions'
And promptly
Fell down the hole.

ANGELA S. HART

Today

Today I put coffee powder in the washing-machine,
Married the goldfish,
Borrowed a fiver off my teddy-bear,
And spoke to my friend Alex on the telephone.

ANGELA S. HART

What Can I Say?

I know, it's true – I've begun
to hide fruit in the boxroom.
Oranges sprout, bright as Belisha beacons
dotted about the dusty environ.

You try to warn me, stress –
'This is not the right place.
Satsumas belong in the fruitbowl
not in a washbowl or suitcase

and lychees and mangoes taste best
before they grow mould.'
But nuts perch on the dado, bananas
go missing in the commode.

I soothe you with sly words,
'Don't be afraid. When I heard
on the news of a Martian invasion
I took this precaution:

My toothbrush is disguised as a broom
there are tea bags in the toe of my boot
and (shush) I've stored the fruit
where it's safe in the boxroom.'

CICELY HERBERT (*b.* 1937)

Reactive Depression

The World is crying,
Sobbed a broken umbrella,
Under the weather.

MARY O'DWYER

Door

He was sad
he was low so low
he was finished
he painted
he painted his last picture

silently bid his goodbyes
and walked out through the door
later
decades later
the gallery attendant
who for years sat beside
beside this last painting
a masterpiece
his favourite
his friend
strange subject
a door
rich in colour
rich in warmth
rich in hue
dazzling shimmering
but
he was sad
he was low so low
he noticed the keyhole
and peered through
secretly
each night
and noticed
and saw
a speck
a figure
far away
a figure painting
a figure waving
he kept
his secret
then one day
silently bid his goodbyes
and walked out through the door.

PATRICK McMANUS (*b.* 1939)

She Thought

She thought
of him
often
especially
when
sticking pins
into
clay figures
sometimes
she also
tarred and feathered
them
before firing.

PATRICK McMANUS

Frozen Falls

We are the frozen people,
the subhuman, mis-shaped people.

We'd like to throw ourselves
into the river, merge with the sea

but our parents
were winds

which slapped our cheeks
until they went numb.

We're so thin
we're transparent.

We are too tall,
elongated by icicles.

Some of us don't have faces.
Some of us have clothes but no bodies.

We hang from the rail
waiting to be worn.

We have ethereal names –
Fallen Angel,

Bridalveil,
Virgin's Tears…

PASCALE PETIT (*b.* 1953)

Interference

He walks out from another row
towards dim orange lamps
going nowhere he knows
on uneven wet pavements
in places splashed by cars;

lights show through curtains
many simply blue
with muffled urgent talking, –
watchers mustn't sleep.
He wouldn't waste his time.

He'd rather fight for words
to say the things he needs
to gain a moment's peace.
If only nights like this
would keep their voices down.

Frank Newsum (*b*. 1936)

The Turkish Carpet

No man could have been more unfaithful
To his wife than me;
Scarcely a day passed
That I was not unfaithful to her.
I would be in the living room ostensibly reading or
    writing
When she'd come home from work unexpectedly early
And, popping her head round the door, find me wrapped
    round
A figure of despair.
It would not have been too bad if I'd been wrapped round
Another woman – that would have been infidelity of a
    kind
With which my wife could have coped.
What she could not cope with, try as she did,
Was the infidelity of unhope,
The personal betrayal of universal despair.
When my wife called to me from the living-room door
Tremblingly ajar, with her head peering round it –
The paintwork studded with headwounds and
    knuckleprints –
Called to me across the red, red grass of home –
The Turkish Carpet –
Which her gay mother had given us as a wedding
    present

(And on which our children had so often played
Dolls' houses on their hands and knees
And headstands and cartwheels and dances,
And on which we ourselves had so often made love),
I clutched my despair to my breast
And with brutality kissed it – Sweet Despair –
Staring red-eyed down at *The Turkish Carpet.*
O my dear husband, will you not be faithful to me?
Have I not given you hope all the days of my life?

PAUL DURCAN (*b.* 1944)

Bagpipes

The bagpipes on the wall began to skirl
the minute she reversed out the drive.
She took with her nothing but her spaniel
and the walnut clock, but they were enough
to convince him she was gone for good.
He stood watching as she swerved away,
out towards the sheep-encrusted headland
where she'd sat every day and painted
portraits of the waves, but today he knew
she wouldn't stop there, was only going
to skid a goodbye, before booting it south
to somewhere he wouldn't be. The bagpipes
droned on, needing no mouth to rouse them.
There was more than one set, clearly –
he'd gatecrashed a bagpipers' convention
in his own home, that was no home now.
He started to scream his accompaniment.
He threw a few mugs at the wall
and took the poker to the mirror.
Beneath it, the voodoo mask was laughing
like he always knew it would. She'd bought it.

She would never take that with her.
He looked at it, and ran at the window.
The bagpipes drowned out the breaking glass.

MATTHEW SWEENEY (*b.* 1952)

The Angel that presided o'er my birth

The Angel that presided o'er my birth
Said, 'Little creature, form'd of Joy & Mirth,
Go love without the help of any Thing on Earth.'

WILLIAM BLAKE (1757–1827)

'Madman' I have been call'd…

'Madman' I have been call'd: 'Fool' they call thee.
I wonder which they Envy, Thee or Me?

WILLIAM BLAKE

Madman

Every child has a madman on their street:
The only trouble about our madman is that he's *our* father.

PAUL DURCAN (*b.* 1944)

About How Many?

About one in six.
What kind of people?
People like us.
Who hasn't wanted
to scream the house down?
Felt there was no point
carrying on?
Sat day-dreaming
at place of employment?
Wouldn't be human
if you hadn't.
Why do five million
people per annum
visit their doctor?...
More working days lost
than flu and bad backs.
All walks of life —
executives, soldiers,
old-age pensioners
(hommes de lettres?).
'Different'? 'Odd'?
Require reassurance.
Occupational
and industrial
therapy units
help, as can Fine Art,
Music and Drama.
Tolerance, patience,
talk freely to them,
build warm relaxed
relationships with them.

PETER READING (*b*. 1946)

The Euphemisms

Crackers, Potty, Loony, Bonkers,
Nutty, Screwy, Ga-Ga, Dull,
Strange, Do-Lally, Dopey, Silly,
Touched, A Bit M., Up the Pole,

Zany, Crazy, Dotty, Batty,
Round the Bend, Remedial, Slow,
Cranky, Turned, Moonstruck, Quixotic,
Odd, Beside Oneself, Loco,

Rambling, Giddy, Flighty, Crackbrained,
Soft, Bewildered, Off One's Head,
Wandering, Wild, Bereft of Reason,
Daft, Distracted, Unhingèd;

Attributes of Simple Simons,
Asses, Owls, Donkeys, Mules,
Nincompoops, Wiseacres, Boobies,
Noodles, Numskulls, Gawks, Tomfools,

Addle/Silly/Chuckle/Dunder/
Sap/Bone/Block/Thick/Muddle/Crack-
Heads, The E.S.N., The Balmy,
Silly Billies, Dunces, Jack-

Asses, Dullards, Merry Andrews,
Mooncalves, at least one MP,
Vauxhall Workers (and Execs), Clods,
Paisleyites, Twerps, Plaid Cymru…

PETER READING

ha ha

ha ha
hee hee
help help
me me

KAREN DAVIES (*b.* 1961)

from Jubilate Agno

Fragment 'C', lines 19–33

For there is a mystery in numbers.
For One is perfect and good being at unity in himself.
For Two is the most imperfect of all numbers.
For every thing infinitely perfect is Three.
For the Devil is two being without God.
For he is an evil spirit male and female.
For he is called the Duce by foolish invocation on that
    account.
For Three is the simplest and best of all numbers.
For Four is good being square.
For Five is not so good in itself but works well in
    combination.
For Five is not so good in itself as it consists of two and
    three.
For Six is very good consisting of twice three.
For Seven is very good consisting of two compleat
    numbers.
For Eight is good for the same reason and propitious to
    me Eighth of March 1761 hallelujah.
For Nine is a number very good and harmonious.

For I prophecy that men will learn the use of their
    knees.
For every thing that can be done in that posture (upon the
    knees) is better so done than otherwise.
For I prophecy that they will understand the
    blessing and virtue of the rain.
For rain is exceedingly good for the human body.
For it is good therefore to have flat roofs to the
    houses, as of old.
For it is good to let the rain come upon the naked body
    unto purity and refreshment.

CHRISTOPHER SMART (1722–71)

The Leaf

Behind me a pattering along the path
Yet when I turned to see what dog was following
It was only a tiny brown leaf
Skipping along from last summer
From a year ago last spring even,
Detached and crisp now in the March breezes
Following me intently while all about it
None of its brothers either stirred or moved.

One leaf had followed me along the path.

St Francis Hospital 1979

HARRY FAINLIGHT (1935–82)

A Lesson

for Linda

Teacher paces out
The afternoon

Note this.

Note that.

Learn by heart
For Monday

One child
Pounced on explains
'Seagulls talk to me.'

A controlled burst
Of laughter
From the class

'Oh yes
And what do they say?'

'It's in seagull,'
The child replies
Then adding patiently
'And it's no good
In English – doesn't rhyme!'

More laughter
But less this time.

KEVIN McCANN

In the Ocean

Mentally, I have begun to pack.
And the scratching of my head
Is like gnawing into my being. I have packed:
The books which will sustain me.
My soul which will torture the sea.
My hair, my teeth and my mind and body.

I have begun to travel
In no man's land.
I'm looking forward to arriving.

Now I've arrived on the beach.
And I'm listening to the ocean.
Going forward and backward,
Forever journeying and not being.

I don't want to return,
At home there will be only Me.
I can't let these treasures go.

The beach does not have sand,
Instead there are rocks and mountains
And the air is cold as ice.
I wish to go on a boat,
Drift aimlessly forget the toil of
Life and stay surrounded by seagulls.
Who will say good day good gosh.

FATMA DURMUSH (*b.* 1959)

Sea

These waters would kill me.
Only fish can survive
in that boiling inferno
or you can see a bird dive
into a salty furrow.
Roof after roof collapses
of transient slaty houses
and suddenly the white horses
rear hoof after hoof
beating the sky away.

IAIN CRICHTON SMITH (*b.* 1928)

I Used to Be a Girl

One day my step-father decided to strangle me.
He took care of me, then.
He took me then.
He had had me ever since we moved into his house.
He took care of me, then.
My mother said I was lucky.
Not all step-fathers
love their step-daughters.

To strangle me was fine. I did indeed
miss the bus. I did indeed
have sand in my schoolbag. I did indeed
forget to learn my rhymes. I did indeed
fail to be good, yes I failed.
My mother said I was lucky.
Not all step-fathers care.

No, I did not mind at all
being strangled.
I only felt wrong doing him a favour.

My mother was standing by, watching,
her hands held out
ready to catch me later. Later.
She was going to catch me.
I knew I could trust her.

I looked at her face then I looked at his,
they merged into a blur of mist and cloud,
only their eyes peeked through like beams, hot rays
making my mouth feel dry and sore.

I could not stop thinking
about the day before, I saw it all,
the way he handled me. He was saying
I was not to be scared.
He was saying he needed me.
He washed his congealed milk out of my hair,
just in time. I told my mother
I was wet because my baby brother
had pissed into my face.
We all laughed.

I am here now. Still here. I am looking
forward to the final blow.
I am indeed looking forward,
into the future. I am lucky
I do not have a daughter. I would find it
hard to hold my hands out ready to catch her.

IFIGENIJA SIMONOVIC (*b.* 1953)
Translated by Anthony Rudolf and the author

Bank Holiday Monday

I'm driven out of my house.
I investigate the River Crane to see if it's good for suicide.
It's full and swift, smooth and brown today
With a bottle bouncing at the weir.
How long can that go on?
It seems cold.
I am appalled.
It's not for me, no place for me.
No place for me.

Upstream a willow scores a delicate surface pattern with
    fronds.
The old apple tree opposite is dull with the labour of
    growing apples,
Its white and pink and new green glory gone.
The strip of wild garden, one year so dug up and mauled
Is glowing flush with green now.
Who has done all that planting
On this no one's patch of ground?

The green, the greens surprise me,
The greens and the dandelion heads.
A glimpse, a glimpse surprises and shocks.
The pain goes fleetingly –
Enough to go back home.
Oh gods that be
I wish I could see.

BARBARA SAUNDERS (*b.* 1937)

Crocuses

And is her father with her on the lawn?
Absolutely not.
She needs to be quite alone.
And what is she drinking, on the lawn?
Hot tea.
And what is she writing?
Things that have made her angry.
And has a certain bunch of flowers
made her angry?
Yes.
He stepped out
into the sunlight,
still in his nightclothes,
and made his way
down the hill
to the orchard.
Her first gold crocuses
were pushing up like fish
(she wanted *no one* to see them)
between striped wasps on plums.

And what sharp implement
was he carrying down with him?
Scissors.
And if he were to cut himself –
remember he's an old man now –
would she come running down the bank with sheets
to stanch the bleeding?
No, she would not.
And will she forgive him?
Never.

SELIMA HILL (*b.* 1945)

from Song

from *Death's Jest Book, or The Fool's Tragedy*
The Deaths. One with a scythe, who has stood sentinel, now sings

Although my old ear
   Hath neither hammer nor drum,
Methinks I can hear
   Living skeletons come.
The cloister re-echoes the call,
   And it frightens the lizard,
And, like an old hen, the wall
Cries 'cluck! cluck! back to my gizzard;
   ''Tis warm, though it's stony,
   'My chickens so bony.'
So come let us hide, each with his bride,
For the wicked are coming who have not yet died.

THOMAS LOVELL BEDDOES (1803–49)

The Owl and the Pussycat

But mother I was only two
And probably very fond of you
When you sent me away
For a year and a day
To the land where the madness grew.

NIKKI GREEN (*b.* 1966)

Villanelle of the Suicide's Mother

Sometimes I almost go hours without crying,
Then I feel if I don't, I'll go insane.
It can seem her whole life was her dying.

She tried so hard, then she was tired of trying;
Now I'm tired, too, of trying to explain.
Sometimes I almost go hours without crying.

The anxiety, the rage, the denying;
Though I never blamed her for my pain,
It can seem her whole life was her dying,

And mine was struggling to save her: prying,
Conniving: it was the chemistry in her brain.
Sometimes I almost go hours without crying.

If I said she was easy, I'd be lying;
The lens between her and the world was stained:
It can seem her whole life was her dying

But the fact, the *fact*, is stupefying:
Her absence tears at me like a chain.
Sometimes I almost go hours without crying.
It can seem her whole life was her dying.

C.K. WILLIAMS (*b.* 1936)

The Second Admission

The fly is evil I must kill it
The red geraniums outside are Satanic
A black cat has arrived in my room
I must choke it to death

My parents are talking about me
Plotting to get rid of me
The G.P. will soon be called

Don't want to visit a mental hospital
Must tidy my flat immediately
Must convince her that I'm sane

JOHN TENNANT (*b.* 1953)

Had we our senses...

Had we our senses
But perhaps 'tis well they're not at Home
So intimate with Madness
He's liable with them

Had we the eyes within our Head –
How well that we are Blind –
We could not look upon the Earth –
So utterly unmoved –

EMILY DICKINSON (1830–86)

Broken Eggs

Blake was mad. Clare was mad. Plath was mad. I'm
O.K. at the moment. I don't think crows
slouch like scavenging border guards. That God's
abandoned the game. That, stripped of reason,
we see. If only you'd glimpsed those poor sods
rocking themselves to some dark place who knows

where, dribble gunging their lips, stiff with crime
and refusal, you'd know what fucking treason
spills from intellectuals, hungry to hang
like limpets on those quaking souls who sang
without hope.

And me, too. I'll pound my rhetoric
grimace to order, take my squashed place
in the hall of mirrors, out on the edge…

The fact is that when your mind flops off track
you might get free enough to fall apart.

And no blazing ladders into the clouds,
no field mice scarcely twitching the long grass,
no small bright wound can put you together,
put you together, put you together
again.

PETER PEGNALL (*b.* 1949)

Arriving Early

You are let in by
a tense woman who
asks you to help with
the washing up.

You follow her past
bowls of nuts and
carefully placed
floor cushions.

She tells you she is a sculptor
working in wire mesh and

artificial hair.
Nobody else turns up.

It begins to dawn on you
you've come to the
wrong flat.

She reaches for the carving knife
and expertly dices celery
no one will eat.

It's time you made a volunteer
trip to the off-licence.

JOE ASSER (*b*. 1964)

Don't Flinch

There's this depressed commuter
standing unnaturally close to
the edge of the platform.

As the tracks begin to rumble
you steel yourself for the fact
that if he really does jump
you won't under any circumstances
close your eyes.

JOE ASSER

Sunday Morning in Putney

Five mushrooms clustered in a tufted dell,
The tintinnabulations of a single lacquered bell,
An ochre mist subsides; Laetitia is not well.

CHRIS RAWLINSON (*b.* 1947)

I Am Vertical

But I would rather be horizontal.
I am not a tree with my root in the soil
Sucking up minerals and motherly love
So that each March I may gleam into leaf,
Nor am I the beauty of a garden bed
Attracting my share of Ahs and spectacularly painted,
Unknowing I must soon unpetal.
Compared with me, a tree is immortal
And a flower-head not tall, but more startling,
And I want the one's longevity and the other's daring.

Tonight, in the infinitesimal light of the stars,
The trees and flowers have been strewing their cool odors.
I walk among them, but none of them are noticing.
Sometimes I think that when I am sleeping
I must most perfectly resemble them –
Thoughts gone dim.
It is more natural to me, lying down.
Then the sky and I are in open conversation,
And I shall be useful when I lie down finally:
Then the trees may touch me for once, and the flowers
    have time for me.

SYLVIA PLATH (1932–63)

The Halls of Bedlam

Forewarned of madness:
In three days' time at dusk
The fit masters him.

How to endure those days?
(Forewarned is foremad)
'– Normally, normally.'

He will gossip with children,
Argue with elders,
Check the cash account.

'I shall go mad that day –'
The gossip, the argument,
The neat marginal entry.

His case is not uncommon,
The doctors pronounce;
But prescribe no cure.

To be mad is not easy,
Will earn him no more
Than a niche in the news.

Then to-morrow, children,
To-morrow or the next day
He resigns from the firm.

His boyhood's ambition
Was to become an artist –
Like any City man's.

To the walls and halls of Bedlam
The artist is welcome –
Bold brush and full palette.

Through the cell's grating
He will watch his children
To and from school.

'Suffer the little children
To come unto me
With their Florentine hair!'

A very special story
For their very special friends –
They burst in the telling:

Of an evil thing, armed,
Tap-tapping on the door,
Tap-tapping on the floor,
'On the third day at dusk.'

Father in his shirt-sleeves
Flourishing a hatchet –
Run, children, run!

No one could stop him,
No one understood;
And in the evening papers...

(Imminent genius,
Troubles at the office,
Normally, normally,
As if already mad.)

ROBERT GRAVES (1895–1985)

Riddym Ravings
(the mad woman's poem)

de fus time dem kar me go a Bellevue
was fit di dactar an de lanlord operate
an tek de radio outa mi head
troo dem sieze de bed
weh did a gi mi cancer
an mek mi talk to nobady
ah di same night wen dem trow mi out fi no pay de rent
mi haffi sleep outa door wid de Channel One riddym box
an de D.J. fly up eena mi head
mi hear im a play seh

Eh, Eh,
no feel no way
town is a place dat ah really kean stay
dem kudda – ribbit mi han
eh – ribbit mi toe
mi waan go a country go look mango

fah wen hungry mek King St. pavement
bubble an dally in front a mi yeye
an mi foot start wanda falla fly
to de garbage pan eena de chinaman backlat
dem nearly chap aff mi han eena de butcha shap
fi de piece a ratten poke
ah de same time de mawga gal in front a mi
drap de laas piece a ripe banana
an mi – ben dung – pick i up – an nyam i
a dat time dem grab mi an kar mi back a Bellevue
dis time de dactar an de lanlord operate
an tek de radio plug outa mi head
den sen mi out, seh mi alright
but – as ah ketch back outa street
ah push een back de plug
an ah hear mi D.J. still a play, seh

Eh, Eh,
no feel no way
town is a place dat ah really kean stay
dem kudda – ribbit mi han
eh – ribbit mi toe
mi waan go a country go look mango

Ha Haah… Haa

wen mi fus come a town
mi use to tell everybady 'mawnin'
but as de likkle rosiness gawn outa mi face
nobady nah ansa mi
silence tun rags roun mi bady
in de mids a all de dead people dem
a bawl bout de caast of livin
an a ongle one ting tap mi fram go stark raving mad
a wen mi siddung eena Parade
a tear up newspaper fi talk to
sometime dem roll up
an tun eena one a Uncle But sweet saaf
yellow heart breadfruit
wid piece a roas saalfish side a i
an if likkle rain jus fall
mi get cocanat rundung fi eat i wid
same place side a weh de country bus dem pull out
an sometime mi a try board de bus
an de canductor bwoy a halla out seh
'dutty gal, kum affa de bus'
ah troo im no hear de riddym eena mi head
same as de tape weh de bus driva a play, seh

Eh, Eh,
no feel no way
town is a place dat ah really kean stay
dem kudda – ribbit mi han
eh – ribbit mi toe
mi waan go a country go look mango

so country bus, ah beg yuh
tek mi home
to de place, where I belang

an di dutty bway jus run mi aff

Well, dis mawnin, mi start out pon Spanish Town Road,
fah mi deh go walk go home a country
fah my granny use to tell mi how she walk fram wes
come a town
come sell food
an mi waan ketch home befo dem put de price pon i'
but mi kean go home dutty?
fah mi parents dem did sen mi out clean
Ah!
see wan stanpipe deh!
so mi strip aff all de crocus bag dem
an scrub unda mi armpit
fah mi hear de two mawga gal dem laas nite
a laugh an seh
who kudda breed smaddy like me?
a troo dem no know seh a pure nice man
weh drive car an have gun
visit my piazza all dem four o'clock a mawnin
no de likkle dutty bwoy dem weh mi see dem a go
        home wid
but as mi feel de clear water pon mi bady
no grab dem grab mi
an is back eena Bellevue dem kar mi
seh mi mad an a bade naked a street
well dis time de dactar an de lanlord operate
an dem tek de whole radio fram outa mi head
but wen dem tink seh mi unda chloroform
dem put i dung careless
an wen dem gawn
mi tek de radio
an mi push i up eena mi belly
fi keep de baby company

fah even if mi nuh mek i
me waan my baby know dis yah riddym yah
fram before she bawn
hear de DJ. a play, seh

Eh, Eh,
no feel no way
town is a place dat ah really kean stay
dem kudda — ribbit mi han
eh — ribbit mi toe
mi waan go a country go look mango

an same time
de dactar an de lanlord
trigger de electric shack
an mi hear de DJ. vice bawl out, seh

Murther
Pull up Missa Operator!

Jean 'Binta' Breeze (*b.* 1956)

Rave On

It was a mad scene man
Gwent Ward early '90s
Psychiactripped off our heads
We did the drugs met the dealers
Chilled out in the smoking room
We were so cool we could stub fags out on our bare arms
It was educational too man
Learnt to fill in sickness benefit forms
Human suffering Man we saw it all
Rape victims abused children battered wives social
    workers stealing kids

Slashed arms screaming every human emotion it was
    intense man
Learnt to stand in a tablet queue
Learnt the side-effects of every drug
Muscle paralysis, paranoia
How to be a zombie
The shaking was the best
Imagine it man
Ten of us zombed out in one smoking room, twenty
legs jittering up and down, twenty hands shaking
spilling coffee trying to get fags into their dry mouths
Man it was a laugh

Jo Harris (*b.* 1970)

Chemical Escape

Shi looked it thi boatul
Shi picked it up
Shi opened it
Shi emptied it oan thi table
Shi coonted 160 pills
Shi spread thum oot
slid thum roond aboot
feelin thur energy
thur buzz, thur control, thur powur
powur ti take hur intae fluid city
shuttin oot grotsville, cuttin oaf torture town.
Shi scooped up thi pills
slowly
an started pittin thum
back in thi boatul

Cecilia Grainger (*b.* 1949)

from *A Season in Hell*: Ravings II

I became a fabulous opera. I saw that all beings have a fatality of happiness. Action is not life, but a way of dissipating some force – an enervation. Morality is the weakness of the brain.

Each being seemed to me to have several *other* lives due to him. This gentleman does not know what he is doing: he is an angel. This family is a pack of dogs. In the presence of several men I have conversed aloud with a moment of one of their other lives. Thus, I have loved a pig.

Not one of the sophistries of madness – the kind of madness that is locked up – have I omitted. I could recite them all; I have the system.

My health was threatened. Terror would come upon me. I would fall into sleeps lasting several days, and on rising would continue the saddest dreams. I was ripe for death, and by a road of dangers my weakness led me to the confines of the world and of Cimmeria, country of darkness and whirlwinds.

To divert the enchantments assembled in my brain, I had to travel. On the sea, which I loved as though it would cleanse me of a defilement, I saw the comforting Cross erect itself. I had been damned by the rainbow. Happiness was my fatality, my remorse, my worm. My life would always be too huge to be devoted to strength and beauty.

Happiness! Its deathly-sweet tooth warned me at cockcrow – *ad matutinum*, at the *Christus venit* – in the darkest cities.

ARTHUR RIMBAUD (1854–91)
Translated by Norman Cameron

The Fabulous Glass

for Blanche Reverchon-Jouve

In my deep Mirror's blindest heart
A Cone I planted there to sprout.
Sprang up a Tree tall as a cloud
And each branch bore a loud-voiced load
Of Birds as bright as their own song;
But when a distant death-knell rang
My Tree fell down, and where it lay
A Centipede disgustingly
Swarmed its quick length across the ground!
Thick shadows fell inside my mind;
Until an Alcove rose to view
In which, obscure at first, there now
Appeared a Virgin and her Child;
But it was horrid to behold
How she consumed that Infant's Face
With her voracious Mouth. Her Dress
Was Black, and blotted all out. Then
A phosphorescent Triple Chain
Of Pearls against the darkness hung
Like a Temptation; but ere long
They vanished, leaving in their place
A Peacock, which lit up the glass
By opening his Fan of Eyes:
And thus closed down my Self-regarding Gaze.

DAVID GASCOYNE (*b.* 1916)

The Song of the Demented Priest

I put those things there. – See them burn.
The emerald the azure and the gold
Hiss and crack, the blues & greens of the world
As if I were tired. Someone interferes
Everywhere with me. The clouds, the clouds are torn
In ways I do not understand or love.

Licking my long lips, I looked upon God
And he flamed and he was friendlier
Than you were, and he was small. Showing me
Serpents and thin flowers; these were cold.
Dominion waved & glittered like the flare
From ice under a small sun. I wonder.

Afterward the violent and formal dancers
Came out, shaking their pithless heads.
I would instruct them but I cannot now, –
Because of the elements. They rise and move,
I nod a dance and they dance in the rain
In my red coat. I am the king of the dead.

JOHN BERRYMAN (1914–72)

The New Arrival

That final day was warm and bright
but he was dark and frozen
in a trenchcoat, damp and caked in clay.
The scissors in his fist was red
blood ran from the remnants of his hair
and his right hand stank of the baby's ass.

He had morphine in the brainpan
brandy in his bark, when he heard
the voices crying fool, fool, fool –
but he was too far out
on a pygmy raft of his own design,
too far out to be no dream.

Money he said – gimme money,
and someone crossed his palm
with paper, a oneway ticket
via first class shock, not negotiable.

First thing he did when he arrived
was buy a map of the new city
which he studied with his good eye.
Soon, he thought. Soon I'll walk.

AIDAN MURPHY (*b*. 1952)

The Starry Night

That does not keep me from having a terrible
need of – shall I say the word – religion. Then I
go out at night to paint the stars.
    VINCENT VAN GOGH in a letter to his brother

The town does not exist
except where one black-haired tree slips
up like a drowned woman into the hot sky.
The town is silent. The night boils with eleven stars
Oh starry starry night! This is how
I want to die.

It moves. They are all alive.
Even the moon bulges in its orange irons

to push children, like a god, from its eye.
The old unseen serpent swallows up the stars.
Oh starry starry night! This is how
I want to die:

into that rushing beast of the night,
sucked up by that great dragon, to split
from my life with no flag,
no belly,
no cry.

ANNE SEXTON (1928–74)

Träume, II

Born with that God-shaped hole in the heart,
he slept badly, woke often. Bad dreams,
he hardly remembered the details,
just the shambles in the street, the muzzle-flash
of a gun in the face, that hollow clunk
at the back of the head as the Henker
turned him off with a drop in the company
of cats and dogs and Jews.
                        That was enough
to be going on with. He slept badly, woke often
on the stroke of sudden, violent death,

and in that way he tackled the ultimate mysteries;

knowing God, going beyond the impenetrable
and, more to the point, returning to testify.
Shot, hanged, butchered, guillotined and unbelieved.

HARRY SMART (b. 1956)

The Cave

I think most people are relieved the first time they
     actually know someone who goes crazy.
It doesn't happen the way you hear about it where the
     person gibbers and sticks to you like an insect:
mostly there's crying, a lot of silence, sometimes someone
     will whisper back to their voices.
All my friend did was sit, at home until they found him,
     then for hours at a time on his bed in the ward,
pointing at his eyes, chanting the same phrase over and
     over 'Too much fire!' he'd say. 'Too much fire!'
I remember I was amazed at how raggedy he looked, then
     annoyed because he wouldn't answer me
and then, when he was getting better, I used to pester him
     to tell me about that fire-thing.
He'd seemed to be saying he'd seen too much and I
     wanted to know too much what
because my obsession then was that I was somehow
     missing everything beyond the ordinary.
What was only real was wrong. There were secrets that
     could turn you into stone,
they were out of range or being kept from me, but my
     friend, if he knew what I meant, wouldn't say,
so we'd talk politics or books or moon over a beautiful girl
     who was usually in the visiting room when we were
who mutilated herself. Every time I was there, new slashes
     would've opened out over her forearms and wrists
and once there were two brilliant medallions on her
     cheeks that I thought were rouge spots
but that my friend told me were scratches she'd put there
     with a broken light bulb when she'd run away the day
     before.
The way you say running away in hospitals is 'eloping.'
     Someone who hurts themself is a 'cutter.'
How could she do it to herself? My friend didn't think
     that was the question.

She'd eloped, cut, they'd brought her back and now she
    was waiting there again,
those clowny stigmata of lord knows what on her, as
    tranquil and seductive as ever.
I used to storm when I'd leave her there with him. She
    looked so vulnerable.
All the hours they'd have. I tormented myself imagining
    how they'd come together,
how they'd tell each other the truths I thought I had to
    understand to live,
then how they'd kiss, their lips, chaste and reverent,
    rushing over the forgiven surfaces.
Tonight, how long afterwards, watching my wife undress,
    letting my gaze go so everything blurs
but the smudges of her nipples and hair and the wonderful
    lumpy graces of her pregnancy,
I still can bring it back: those dismal corridors, the furtive
    nods, the moans I thought were sexual
and the awful lapses that seemed vestiges of exaltations
    I would never have,
but now I know whatever in the mystery I was looking for,
    whatever brute or cloud I thought eluded me,
isn't lost in the frenzy of one soul or another, but next to
    us, in the touch between.
Lying down, fumbling for the light, moving into the
    shadow with my son or daughter, I find it again:
the prism of hidden sorrow, the namelessness of nothing
    and nothing shuddering across me,
and then the warmth, clinging and brightening, the hide,
    the caul, the first mind.

C.K. WILLIAMS (*b.* 1936)

The Intruders

Inside my head
Slivers of wood are lodged.
They prevent messages passing
From one part of my brain
To another.

I hear what you say
And one of my brains understands,
But the others cannot,
Because the wooden blocks
Block the paths of the messages.

I attempt to dislodge these wooden pieces,
Yet the more I try,
The more firmly they become wedged.
Confusion reigns.

They are hurting my head,
They are hurting my thoughts,
They are hurting my feelings,
They are hurting ME.

I am struggling so hard
Not to cry with the pain,
And resolve to strive harder still
To join my brains together
In order to feel whole for ever.

DENISE JONES (*b.* 1951)

Rampton Special Hospital: Arrival

I remember the crossing between fields of oil seed rape
the spider track of a black bus in a sticky yellow web
six jostled passengers
faces borrowed from arctic explorers
the moment before death. I remember.

I remember the carbolic stew that would not digest
but jostled for air at the back of my throat
then the fence, the guards and the one armed barrier
dropping behind as a wire severs a ration of cheese.
And then, I remember, we were inside.

DANIELLE HOPE (*b.* 1958)

Therefore I Will Not Fear

On Rubery Hill the birds do sing,
On Rubery Hill the merry cats can prance,
On Rubery Hill the children dance,
On Rubery Hill the swallows wing
Their way between the wind and sky,
On Rubery Hill the cats cry
Like little lost birds. You can lie
On Rubery Hill and not see no one
But farms and flats and roads and cats
And thunder roars on Rubery Hill but
You won't see the lightning 'cos you're blue
And go to bed at eight or nine
And wake up when the weather's fine
On Rubery Hill on Rubery Hill
Go now to sleep and take your pill.

Who calls the dark cats?
Who the bell?   tolls out of the
Hatch and finds us well?
Who rings the angelus so
We can hear, and angels us,
Too soon to sleep?
Whence comes this
Anxious calm to us, to lower me
To sleep? It's alright, all right,
The sky gathers the light left,
Let all cats sing!

On Rubery Hill the birds call,
On Rubery Hill the flats sparkle,
Change perspective. There are never people
On Rubery Hill, only at night when there
Are choirs of school children, concealed
Noisily, shouting to each other. O, I was
Six months dead, and six months came I alive
I want to suffer, want to leap from the
High hills, as once from a hill near Lucca
I leapt, I will the extremities, not slow
Death on Rubery Hill.

NICHOLAS LAFITTE (1943–70)

Noon Walk on the Asylum Lawn

The summer sun ray
shifts through a suspicious tree.
though I walk through the valley of the shadow
It sucks the air
and looks around for me.

The grass speaks.
I hear green chanting all day.
I will fear no evil, fear no evil
The blades extend
and reach my way.

The sky breaks.
It sags and breathes upon my face.
in the presence of mine enemies, mine enemies
The world is full of enemies.
There is no safe place.

ANNE SEXTON (1928–74)

Ringing the Bells

And this is the way they ring
the bells in Bedlam
and this is the bell-lady
who comes each Tuesday morning
to give us a music lesson
and because the attendants make you go
and because we mind by instinct,
like bees caught in the wrong hive,
we are the circle of the crazy ladies
who sit in the lounge of the mental house
and smile at the smiling woman
who passes us each a bell,
who points at my hand
that holds my bell, E flat,
and this is the grey dress next to me
who grumbles as if it were special
to be old, to be old,
and this is the small hunched squirrel girl
on the other side of me

who picks at the hairs over her lip,
who picks at the hairs over her lip all day,
and this is how the bells really sound,
as untroubled and clean
as a workable kitchen,
and this is always my bell responding
to my hand that responds to the lady
who points at me, E flat;
and although we are no better for it,
they tell you to go. And you do.

ANNE SEXTON

Counting the Mad

This one was put in a jacket,
This one was sent home,
This one was given bread and meat
But would eat none,
And this one cried No No No No
All day long.

This one looked at the window
As though it were a wall,
This one saw things that were not there,
This one things that were,
And this one cried No No No No
All day long.

This one thought himself a bird,
This one a dog,
And this one thought himself a man,
An ordinary man,
And cried and cried No No No No
All day long.

DONALD JUSTICE (*b.* 1925)

I Am

The Asylum, Northampton

I am; yet what I am none cares or knows;
    My friends forsake me like a memory lost;
I am the self-consumer of my woes:
    They rise and vanish in oblivious host,
Like shades in love and death's oblivion lost;
And yet I am, and live with shadows tost

Into the nothingness of scorn and noise,
    Into the living sea of waking dreams,
Where there is neither sense of life nor joys,
    But the vast shipwreck of my life's esteems;
And e'en the dearest – that I loved the best –
Are strange – nay, rather, stranger than the rest.

I long for scenes where man has never trod;
    A place where woman never smiled or wept;
There to abide with my creator, God,
    And sleep as I in childhood sweetly slept:
Untroubling and untroubled where I lie,
The grass below – above the vaulted sky.

JOHN CLARE (1793–1864)

Clare's Jig #43

I'd collected a good jig called 'The Self',
but lilting it last night for Dr Bottle
he chided me, opined it should be *Sylph*,
which is Greek, like much he says, meaning *beetle*.
He chokes the same and gibbets butterflies,
now all your rich men's fashionable rage.
My fellow inmates praise him to the skies,
and like a hawk he scans my every page,
the dumb morris of these poor whopstraw words.
When pressed, a melancholy Johnson said
'Why Sir, we are a nest of singing birds!'
Well I hear boughs breaking inside my head
so listen till the music has to stop,
for like a tree, I'm dying from the top.

IAN DUHIG (*b.* 1954)

Hospital for Defectives

By your unnumbered charities
A miracle disclose,
Lord of the Images, whose love,
The eyelid and the rose
Takes for a language, and today
Tell to me what is said
By these men in a turnip field
And their unleavened bread.

For all things seem to figure out
The stirrings of your heart.
And two men pick the turnips up
And two men pull the cart;

And yet between the four of them
No word is ever said
Because the yeast was not put in
Which makes the human bread.
But three men stare on vacancy
And one man strokes his knees;
What is the meaning to be found
In such dark vowels as these?

Lord of the Images, whose love,
The eyelid and the rose
Takes for a metaphor, today
Beneath the warder's blows,
The unleavened man did not cry out
Or turn his face away;
Through such men in a turnip field
What is it that you say?

THOMAS BLACKBURN (1916–77)

To God

Why have you made life so intolerable
And set me between four walls, where I am able
Not to escape meals without prayer, for that is possible
Only by annoying an attendant. And tonight a sensual
Hell has been put on me, so that all has deserted me
And I am merely crying and trembling in heart
For death, and cannot get it. And gone out is part
Of sanity. And there is dreadful hell within me.
And nothing helps. Forced meals there have been and
    electricity
And weakening of sanity by influence
That's dreadful to endure. And there is Orders
And I am praying for death, death, death,

And dreadful is the indrawing or out-breathing of breath
Because of the intolerable insults put on my whole soul,
Of the soul loathed, loathed, loathed of the soul.
Gone out every bright thing from my mind.
All lost that ever God himself designed.
Not half can be written of cruelty of man, on man,
Not often such evil guessed as between man and man.

IVOR GURNEY (1890–1937)

The Madman Compares God to a Great Light

Sometimes I can lie exposed to this
Huge bright. This is because light
Is a source of warmth, solace of the
Deprived. Outside my personal solarium
I can strain toward the electric bulb

And feel my eyelids turn to blood.
I can believe in the glory of great
Suns behind black clouds. I can even
Go as far as to construct the reverse
Of my desolation. Look! my artefact

Produces angular patterns on the roof
Of my eye – I mean the bright green
Whorls and cicatrices that join to-
gether behind the light. Once, on a
Walk, I found an old bicycle I could

Destroy without destroying the light.
Disused things take the light like I
Take a bath. Regard the light as you
Regard the twisted roots lying above
The ground. Light is that aweful

Organising concept that makes mockery
Of the rage for order, the fine frenzy
For precision. Also, I believe in use-
ful peasants who suck the light, who
Plough the coloured earth, drink rusted

Beer, who tend the differential soils.
(Now my body is wrackt by a minor dis-
comfort, and mind pulled, delicately,
Across the brain cavity, till she is
Taut). I can conceive the peace of God,

The expanded simpleness which like air
Warm water light embraces my every pagan
Part. Enough to stand beneath a tree
That stares upwards as I stare, into
The brightness of grey clouds. Enough

To watch the flickering leaves, the
Damp air, the understanding light.
O I can believe in the glory of great
Suns, great suns behind monstrous clouds:
Walk back into the light as you walk into

The wind; suffer the light as you suffer
The cold air, as you suffer the pricking
Of the gentle rain: Let the sun burn in
His high sky; let the earth receive, let
The chilly moon reflect. From this torment,

From my desolation, I move towards again I move
Towards a state of light I do not understand.

NICHOLAS LAFITTE (1943–70)

To Sleep Perchance to Dream

The robots made and drank
their morning tea
The sleepers sat in opposite
chairs silently
An artifice of intelligence
allowed them to greet
each other
'Hello' said the sleepers
in sand dry voices
void of cover
In the front room where
mechanical things were done
the sleepers eyes were opaque
meaningless save a black
set sun
and the robots' eyes recorded
dreams because we now are one
And the outside world that
couldn't impinge this oblivion
save the rain on a membrane tapping
'bring the washing in'
And the sleepers slept on drifting
through the seascape of
a shipwreck
and the robots reacting found them
a pain in a nervous wreck

NICOLA EAST

Two Anonymous Russian Poems

The following two poems were smuggled out of the Arsenal prison mental hospital in Leningrad by the dissident Victor Fainberg in the early 1970s. They are from a manuscript boook bound in surgical tape which he was given by a thief of honour, who claimed that the poems, which he had written out in one night, were by many hands. The translator, however, believes that they are one person's work.

The voice goes dumb...

The voice goes dumb
   in the telephone receiver
      I go cautiously
         in the sleepy darkness
         and the waves run off far away
      from the walls of the mooring
   carrying the writings of centuries
into the fjord of sadness.

How can I find a spark of reality...

How can I find a spark of reality
in the huge dump of the concrete?
To gather
the dispersed light in spaces,
and flood with it foreign palms?

To capture the visionary ships beyond the seas,
to eavesdrop on the songs of the sand in the desert,
to find the manuscript memory of the earth,
and to read out the infinite name?
To gather my thoughts into the bee's sting,

to see the finality of the sphinx in tears,
to find myself in me,
and with the rib of pyramids
measure the rhythmicality of breathing in the darkness?

Translated by Richard McKane

Voices of Bulgaria

He's found a bear the same size as his mother
and walks about the dayroom holding her.
He calls her Marigold. With velvet ears

he hears the yellow sea below the window
rocking on the sand-bar like a horse
lying on its side, that can't stand up;

or like the parrot that he slept beside:
he wrapped it in a scarf with hearts on it,
to keep it warm, but even then it died...

His heavy hand is resting on her dress,
crushing her dumb sleepy whitened roots
beneath the snow, beside the little villa,

where lost mysterious voices of Bulgaria
are heard among the rabbits, quietly singing...
He grunts and ties his hair into a knot.

The polystyrene granules Marigold
was holding back so long come pouring down
like gold and jewels: *Marigold, my love!*

SELIMA HILL (*b.* 1945)

The Visitors

'This patient was obviously hallucinating as I spoke to her"
(Consultant's note)

There was one in the room, thinking of the sherry
he would have before lunch, rocking slightly in his chair.

There was another opposite him, grey hair falling
across a face like a coy but ravaged schoolgirl.

There were others present to whom she would have
    talked
had he not asked her tedious questions, eyeing her.

They were invisible to him, his ego balanced well,
his libido functioning perfectly, his accountant satisfied.

Sometimes their faces got between her and the desk,
mocking and bony, whispering foul insinuations.

When they advanced too far across the carpet
she wanted to get up and tell them to go away,

but his tight clinical voice held her poised
between the overt grins and the beckoning hands.

In the end, he won, and the others bobbed like balloons
in a corner, unmistakably there, but further away.

At last she was compelled to tell them to go away from
    her,
though she could see them reflected in his glasses,
    waiting.

He asked her questions, and noted down her hesitant
    answers
in a precise hand on a long yellow form.

In the end, he formally ushered her out into the corridor,
the faces, mouthing obscenities, followed in a muddled
    bunch,

crowding with her through the narrow door, escorting
her back to the ward where they settled in like squatters,

one on the end of the bed, some by the locker,
and one who laid his head on her pillow, talking softly

until she fell asleep abruptly, and for a while
the visitors crept away silently or floated gently out,

leaving only the faintest trace of their presence,
like a perfume or a discarded cigarette burning away.

ELIZABETH BARTLETT (*b.* 1924)

Waking in the Blue

The night attendant, a B. U. sophomore,
rouses from the mare's-nest of his drowsy head
propped on *The Meaning of Meaning.*
He catwalks down our corridor.
Azure day
makes my agonized blue window bleaker.
Crows maunder on the petrified fairway.
Absence! My heart grows tense
as though a harpoon were sparring for the kill.
(This is the house for the 'mentally ill'.)

What use is my sense of humor?
I grin at Stanley, now sunk in his sixties,
once a Harvard all-American fullback,
(if such were possible!)
still hoarding the build of a boy in his twenties,
as he soaks, a ramrod
with the muscle of a seal
in his long tub,
vaguely urinous from the Victorian plumbing.
A kingly granite profile in a crimson golf-cap,
worn all day, all night,
he thinks only of his figure,
of slimming on sherbet and ginger ale –
more cut off from words than a seal.

This is the way day breaks in Bowditch Hall at McLean's;
the hooded night lights bring out 'Bobbie,'
Porcellian '29,
a replica of Louis XVI
without the wig –
redolent and roly-poly as a sperm whale,
as he swashbuckles about in his birthday suit
and horses at chairs.

These victorious figures of bravado ossified young.

In between the limits of day,
hours and hours go by under the crew haircuts
and slightly too little nonsensical bachelor twinkle
of the Roman Catholic attendants.
(There are no Mayflower
screwballs in the Catholic Church.)

After a hearty New England breakfast,
I weigh two hundred pounds
this morning. Cock of the walk,
I strut in my turtle-necked French sailor's jersey
before the metal shaving mirrors,

and see the shaky future grow familiar
in the pinched, indigenous faces
of these thoroughbred mental cases,
twice my age and half my weight.
We are all old-timers,
each of us holds a locked razor.

ROBERT LOWELL (1917–77)

Night Garden of the Asylum

An owl's call scrapes the stillness.
Curtains are barriers and behind them
The beds settle into neat rows.
Soon they'll be ruffled.

The garden knows nothing of illness.
Only it knows of the slow gleam
Of stars, the moon's distilling; it knows
Why the beds and lawns are levelled.

Then all is broken from its fullness.
A human cry cuts across a dream.
A wild hand squeezes an open rose.
We are in witchcraft, bedevilled.

ELIZABETH JENNINGS (*b.* 1926)

The Voice of Bobo

i.m. the late Bobo, bull terrier

Everything inside this room is mine.
And everyone inside it has to stay.

It's where I keep my horses and my men,
cooled on summer days by giant fans
whose steady rhythm
calms the anxious mind.

Nor do I want torpor, or docility.
From the very moment I arrive

I like to have each person's full attention,
until a silence is attained so deep

some of you will hear the Voice of Bobo,
when, after having queues of tiresome people

teasing her by blowing down her ear,
she suddenly can't bear it any longer

and starts to bark, as only Bobo can.
Those who hear that precious Voice go forward

to other, smaller rooms, for the Advanced.
Everybody else must stay on here –

here between the land and the sea
where long ago I built this secret palace

balanced on the cliff among the predators
to take advantage of the sweeping views.

Selima Hill (*b.* 1945)

The Happiest Woman Alive

Joy was the happiest woman alive. Two hundred 10p phone calls to her ex-husband in London, until he finally telephoned the hospital long-distance, in despair, begging the nurses to remove all Joy's 10p coins.

'I can't get any sleep, she's ringing at all times of the day and night.'

'We can't stop her using the telephone, Mr Hoskworth', was the reply, although they did, the very next day, carting her off along the corridor to the ECT Dept.

ANGELA S. HART

Ode to a Therapist

He's a psychotherapist
He thinks he's a behaviourist
He's really a misogynist
Should have been a ventriloquist

CHRIS NERNEY (*b.* 1952)

Orpheus in the Underworld

Curtains of rock
And tears of stone,
Wet leaves in a high crevice of the sky:
From side to side the draperies
Drawn back by rigid hands.
And he came carrying the shattered lyre,

And wearing the blue robes of a king,
And looking through eyes like holes torn in a screen;
And the distant sea was faintly heard,
From time to time, in the suddenly rising wind,
Like broken song.

Out of his sleep, from time to time,
From between half-open lips,
Escaped the bewildered words which try to tell
The tale of his bright night
And his wing-shadowed day
The soaring flights of thought beneath the sun
Above the islands of the seas
And all the deserts, all the pastures, all the plains
Of the distracting foreign land

He sleeps with the broken lyre between his hands,
And round his slumber are drawn back
The rigid draperies, the tears and wet leaves,
Cold curtains of rock concealing the bottomless sky.

DAVID GASCOYNE (*b.* 1916)

From One Helpstone Man to Another

'I am! yet what I am who cares, or knows?'

Farmboy's been out a long time, swanning around,
thinks he's 'Lord-love-us' Byron, signs hisself such,
scrawling his gibberish; love letters to that Martha
and Mary, both dead to him. They got his measure,
keeping house in a ditch, under a turn of earth.
Eating grass for a promise is about his mark.

He fits in with the other lunatics, but why they let
them wander; Lazarus-men, in their heads, unhinged
    doors,
doves from a cot, cuckoos more like, useless
in and out like fiddlers elbows. I'd keep them
dosed, give them oakum to pick, honest work
stop their hands weaving too close to the Devil.

He doesn't have a clue. Who is he half the time,
our John, our sainted poet! Head's away woolgathering
in heaven! or the other place, roaming meadows,
up to no good, I'll be bound. They turned his head;
been better off if they'd left him, simple like.
Teaching him his letters, was right daft!

ROBERT COLE (*b.* 1951)

The MIND Day Centre

I feel myself learning from the old lags
Bandura et al, imitative learning.
It's quite a skill, sitting in a chair, staring into space,
I did try reading a book, but got discussed,
when I laughed reading it
heard I was a manic depressive.
No one laughs at the MIND day centre.
Brought a few cans in, got called an alcoholic,
That's definitely against the rules,
the rules they supposedly 'Don't Have'
In the end go to the local pub
Guy there says 'I went in there they wouldn't
let me out'
So, MIND doesn't have labels
Pull the other one, saddens me,
I don't want to learn to be more mentally ill

when I say that, the professional says
'You should hear yourself'
and again uses the language of my oppression
to oppress me She even cynically uses 'user rights'
To take away mine

PAUL KEAN (*b.* 1958)

Therapy Room

Joe's making a stool.
I'm weaving a basket.
Someone's making coffee
Dee says *I can sing*
and she does.
Jane won't make an
ashtray.
Arthur's sulking because
the priest wouldn't re-
christen him *Jesus.*
Jane still won't make
an ashtray, instead
she becomes a dog.
ggrrr Woof woof Woof!
Dogs don't make ashtrays.
Dee's singing the
national anthem.
Arthur blesses me.
Sydney hasn't spoken
all morning, or yesterday
or the day before,
ggrrrr Woof Woof!
Shit said Joe
I'm going to discharge
myself from this place

it's driving me mad.
Realizing what he had
said, he starts to laugh.
I also start to laugh,
the man on my left
(who didn't hear Joe)
starts to laugh as well.
We all laugh
except Sid who wants
to die (and means it).
Then we had coffee.

BILL LEWIS (*b.* 1953)

We Call This the Day Room

Have you ever been here? A full
empty day high as a room,
grey, bland – a whole tall
square of air to inhale
before another bed-time.

Can you see our view?
Look at the little willow and the black
trees like hands, severe, cut back.
See the paint peel
on the pale disregarded gazebo.

Do you like jigsaws? This one's
all there, according to Gilbert. He's normally
an accountant, but I have my suspicions
about the big hole in the sky.
Still, it beats watching TV all day.
(Odd, how each day just one day's worth of new happens.)
The empty sky is grey, and the lawns:

sometimes people stroll there, walk
their dogs through the courtyard, or talk.
It's hard to keep making them all perform.
Did you see the corridor?
I don't much care for the décor:
mosaic mares can stare up from the floor
by the hatch where we wait for our medication.
In the wallpaper sometimes I see Buddhas or toads
    seeking satori.

CHARLES JOHNSON (*b.* 1942)

The Day Room

from Kendal Ward, Rainhill Mental Hospital

I

Many are nonplussed
By the unexpected behaviour of their clothes
And have mislaid forever
The art of wearing the face.

Gums wedged tight or mouths
Locked open in a scream that travels inward
Homelessly:

Here we all are on your holy mountain.

It's a little bit nippy up here on the mountain
For some are shivering, never
Stop shivering, also

Unseasonably warm. That man
Is caked with lava, head to hip.

2

Come in, come in,
Don't shut the door.
Take care your feet
Don't touch the floor.

Come on, come on.
Avoid the wall.
Whatever you do
Don't breathe at all.

Stand back, stand back.
What is it? Ask
But whisper through
Your cotton mask.

Back out. Make sure
The door is closed.
Now wash your hands
And burn your clothes.

3

Joan's mouth is a crematorium.
Six years after her husband died
It burns and bleeds and weeps, she cannot beat
His flaring ashes down with her tongue.

All in the mind, and pain
(What was said? What left unsaid?)
A child of the mind
That eats the mother.

The widow is burned alive.

4

Where cigarettes are the entire economy
Domestic policy is locker-love.
Pink stones to arm the military,
White coats for the judiciary,
One hall in hell for all of the above.

5

The male nurses, without exception,
Corpulent, good-natured,
Moustachioed forty-year-olds.
Five of them. How can this be?

They must have a club where they stand and swap
Rounds and jokes and mistakes and moustaches,
Taking each other's paunches
Like a pulse.

6

Our road's a green carbolic corridor
Off which on certain days the sun
Ripens in small groves. In one

I found her crying because she had lost her lipstick
And, so she said, her bones.

The sun poured down.

We found the lipstick, couldn't find the bones.

7

Unspeakable blue
Observed
Through unbreakable glass.

How long have those humanoid beech-limbs,
Their green-dust glaze a parody of spring,
Aped inmates? Patients here
Slept on hay and this afternoon
We queue like sheepish children
For the tablet trolley,
Candy counter that won't divert
The all-day double-honking donkey bray
Of Josie,
Without mind. Or is it
Meaning, is it
What we call gladness in the natural world
As the faint cry of those gulls
Dancing over the kitchen pickings:

A wheeling above
The leavings, mirth
In what she might have been?

8

Pat threw herself away
From babies, from
A seventh floor. Foetus-coiled
She sleeps all day
On two sun-coloured plastic chairs,
Snug by the mother-warmth
Of the radiator.

9

Reg was a Ship's Officer,
Blue Funnel, Ellermans.

Alert on the bridge and likewise
Scholarly in the chartroom,

He wheeled great cargoes
Through the Southern seas.

Struck off the pool, he slumps
Blindly on the windowsill,

His head plunged into his arms
That are guiding nothing.

10

One sits fluttering, fluttering.
Poor, pale moth stuck through with a pin.

One seeks me out to whisper
Extraordinary confidences
Concerning the holy ghost
And a computer. One

Rages up and down the day room
Shouting, 'It's shite.' Everyone's right.

11

The evening canteen
Is where like minds meet.
Eruptions of senile fisticuffs,
Dancing and even
Love I've seen:

One childishly sprawled
On another's knee,
Sucked kisses with cigarettes
Endangering the endearments.

Behind a partition,
The healthful sane are playing badminton.
The shuttlecock soars to heaven like a searchlight,
Drifts to the earth like snow.

Our side
Has a stout Edwardian billiard table,
Permanently sheeted,
Reserved for the diversions of the dead.

12

Many streets in the hospital,
'The largest of any kind
In Europe' when it was built and many
Minds within the mind.

'The shifting population
Of a grid-iron city.'
Pathetic co-operations and courtesies,
Hunger and pity.

This is your holy mountain,
Your shallow grave.
When nothing's left this is what's left
To save.

KIT WRIGHT (*b.* 1944)

Dolor

I have known the inexorable sadness of pencils,
Neat in their boxes, dolor of pad and paper-weight,
All the misery of manilla folders and mucilage,
Desolation in immaculate public places,

Lonely reception room, lavatory, switchboard,
The unalterable pathos of basin and pitcher,
Ritual of multigraph, paper-clip, comma,
Endless duplication of lives and objects.
And I have seen dust from the walls of institutions,
Finer than flour, alive, more dangerous than silica,
Sift, almost invisible, through long afternoons of tedium,
Dropping a fine film on nails and delicate eyebrows,
Glazing the pale hair, the duplicate grey standard faces.

THEODORE ROETHKE (1908–63)

Heard in a Violent Ward

In heaven, too,
You'd be institutionalized.
But that's all right, –
If they let you eat and swear
With the likes of Blake,
And Christopher Smart,
And that sweet man, John Clare.

THEODORE ROETHKE

The Prisoner

Take a deep breath
Then open the door
Step slowly outside
You've done it before
Take a deep breath
Hold your head high

Walk a few steps
You're not going to die
Take a deep breath
Walk up the street
Your heart will beat faster
And then miss a beat
Take a deep breath
Walk slowly back
Try not to panic
You'll soon have the knack
Take a deep breath
Step back inside
Congratulate yourself
Because you have tried
Take a deep breath
Then close the door
Try again tomorrow
You've done it before.

PATRICIA PRATT

To Zimmer

The lines of life are various; they diverge and cease
Like footpaths and the mountains' utmost ends.
What here we are, elsewhere a God amends
With harmonies, eternal recompense and peace.

FRIEDRICH HÖLDERLIN (1770–1843)
Translated by Michael Hamburger

Nightnurse

She is stately and walks slowly
Like a New Orleans funeral
Sways to vast noiseless rhythms
Oh my, oh my, oh my
And she holds the keys
To kingdoms of pain.

Leck, Strick, and Munting,
May the Good Sister keep you
Guard and protect you
From pentecostal dark
From she who sways slowly;
May the dripfeed not fail you

– Do not cry out!
Your moans make her glad –
May morphine cocoon you
May pethidine soothe you
Oh daytime come quickly
For the Nightnurse is mad.

Leck, you once had many words
Till winter frost
Rose through your brain
Now you have forgotten who said
He would rather be arteriosclerotic
Than Lord of Lower Egypt.

Strick, you are dreaming.
The beadle asks your father's height
To measure him for a coffin;
But sorry, no funeral for seven days.
Still, for a sly consideration,
Something can be arranged.

(Here nothing can be arranged,
Says the Nightnurse,
And there is no consideration).

And meanwhile, what of Munting?
Munting cannot remember.

Leck, Strick, and Munting
May cocaine protect you
May Angel Largactil
Bring Light to your Dark;
In the purgatory of your half-sleep
Good and Dead are all the same
Death comes but once
Oh my, oh my, oh my
But night and the Nightnurse
Will soon be round again.

MARTIN SONENBERG

The Hand of God

The hand of God comes to me with a bottle
and the label on the bottle says take two,
Nitrazepam, Temazepam, and sleep.
Who says faith is difficult today

and who would not be grateful for it,
who profess no need? Only a fool.
I take the medicine God has handed out
and, magically, I sense it start to work;

the sedatives are swimming in my veins,
a shoal of favourite words beyond control,
a lustre, velvet, plush and shimmering,
a bump of cushioned nerves, all warm and murmuring,

the world assumes a quiet pose, test cricket
on TV, the cosy hush of snooker rooms
and peaceful bars: Temazepam, Nitrazepam;
they hold me softly as an evening prayer

when all distress has broken down
to worship, adoration, and the soul can rise,
the body spiral out of sight below.
The sky is black and beautiful again

and I'm in love; Temazepam, Nitrazepam and God;
motet, chorale, my precious opiates all,
my liberty, my faithful champions
that lift me, oh so gently, out of hell.

HARRY SMART (*b*. 1956)

Not a Buttercup

There is Celandine
In the hospital grounds
And the nurses ask
'Am I well?'
There is Celandine
In the hospital grounds
But who the hell can I tell?

… Quietly, by the Blackthorn,
That everyone sees and knows,
With the white and nebulous

Dreamy height
Of its flowering boughs.

There is Celandine
In the hospital grounds
And the nurses ask
'Am I well?'
There is Celandine,
In the hospital grounds,
But who am I going to tell?

CAROL BATTON (*b.* 1951)

The Whispering

An occasional word leaps out
from the steady, manic stream.

I put my ear to the bank,
the frail baton of light

that any moment might give
the meaning beneath the surface.

I'm still here, trying,
trying to understand.

And you're still there,
unintelligible,

on the other side of the glass.

PAUL HENRY (*b.* 1959)

The Visitors

The women of my earliest years
fill this room's empty bay
without warning –

     Brown Helen,
Catrin Sands, Gwyneth Blue,
Nightingale Ann…

    Their songs
return to a stranger's hand
the keys to all past tenancies,

Heulwen, Dwynwen, Bron Y Llan…

I lie back, let them haunt,
the soft pulse of their lips
against the stone wall I've become,

Heather, Geta, Prydwen Jane…

listen hard across the dark
as their voices fade again,

Edith Smart, St Julia…

sleep with the bedroom door ajar
in case they should drift back in.

PAUL HENRY

Daycentre Romance

Holding hands in the Bunny Park,
looking over our shoulders
for off-duty nurses;
incognito cappuccinos
at the pavement café –
you in your dark glasses,
me with my head in a book.
Making as if
we hardly knew each other
in the daycentre common room:
secret glances
through a rollies and tea-steam haze.
Stockpiling condoms
against love's improvidence,
we'd clear out both dispensers
in the ladies and the gents.

Doomed from the start
our romance
watched from every window.
Written up in doctors' notes
before we knew it was love.
Even depo-provera
couldn't qualify your terror,
nor mine by what we meant
to each other.

Lingering for a lunch-hour glimpse
at the playground railings,
you could not remember
the colour

of your daughter's eyes.
So are all our children lost
that we're disallowed to keep,
and our love
as futureless as dust.

RAY WILLMOTT (*b*. 1951)

The Game

The game
chasing the
gamekeeper
would be
wiser
not to
crow.

IMMA MADDOX (*b*. 1955)

The Shadow-Board

When the young man with the rapt
face of a saint came to do Pottery
I was his teacher, barely a stage ahead
and two years younger. 'He's schiz
and a bit depressed' said my Senior.
'Make sure of the tools
and chain your scissors.'
'You must wedge the clay
on the plaster slab' I told him.
Shoulder to shoulder we stood

not talking because of his voices
his arms white as a girl's
but muscular. He did it again
and again, blank-faced,
without a question.
'Your uniform's splashed.
Where are your cuffs?'
said my Senior.

Then I took him beyond
in case he lost interest
folded his hands round the heavy
kneaded ball of clay and threw it
hard down on the spinning centre.
We coned it up to the rise and fall
of a phallus. 'Now' I said
'put your thumbs down.
Open the clay like a flower
with both your hands.'

'He won't be coming' she said,
right by my elbow. I was making
a vase and it went off-centre.
'He went down to the railway line
early this morning.
That's when they do it.
Don't blame yourself,
there's a long history.'

I hung the tools on the shadow-board
and locked the cupboard.

JILL BAMBER

Gwutt

green dot.
trainers –
wings.
there. mi
unicorn

HEBRON WACHENJE (1972–96)

Speak to Me

I'm going to stop.
I'm going to start again.
I'm going to make strategic little piles
of things like cigarettes and sugar-cubes,
and bantams' eggs, and cubes of cattle-cake,
and range them, along your route,

until you notice them;
and then I'm going to balance
slightly larger things,
like fish, or fruit, or tulips, on my head,
whispering as I walk: *Speak to me,*
whispering *Speak to me please.*

SELIMA HILL (*b.* 1945)

By Torchlight

The touch of a torch slithering along my thigh must have woken me. I didn't open my eyes. It was a hot night, it was always hot in here. The window was open the regulation 6 inches. I had kicked the green quilt away. Tiny beads of sweat were popping on my upper lip. I wore no clothes. I slowed down my breathing. The heat of the torch was burning into my pubic hair.

My whole body squirmed away, played over and over again the simple movement of reaching out and drawing the cotton quilt across. I was held in the beam, seemingly unaware. I peeped under lowered lashes. He was standing inside the door, the windowed door with the curtains on the outside, the door without a lock. He was four feet from my bed.

In daylight he made me uncomfortable… anglepoise man. I would watch him as he walked the corridors. I could sometimes see the ghost of the eight year old he had been superimposed on his mean features. He was a boy who liked to play soldiers. As he walked, his ghost would settle softly on him, forcing his arms to stick out at bizarre angles to his body. They would swing to and fro, carrying his whole body forward on their momentum, hard heels hitting the floor, head high, buttocks steely with tension. Some one must have told this little boy that he shat gold bars. I had his number. I watched him then, he watched me now.

I shut my eyes, hoping the movement had not been noticed, hoping I had not drawn attention to myself. I shut my eyes as if shutting them would render me invisible to him.

He was a stickler for the rules. He needed them to keep himself on the straight and narrow, fearing that any let up would allow an opening for his venomous loneliness to leak out and harm someone. The vulnerable 'someones' he looked after, patronized every day. He had no room for compassion, especially if one of them said 'I want, I need, I hurt…'. 'More than my job's worth', he would say if they wanted the rules bent a little. He could not afford to crack.

He was on night duty… he was even creepier after dark… Fear was making my breath fast. There was an almost imperceptible movement in the beam. My guts throbbed and rose to my throat, my knees wanted to jerk up to my chest. Not a muscle moved. He was breathing heavier. Or was that me? He was standing closer, three feet from the bed. He moved no further. He wasn't stupid. It was the torch that moved, that hot-eyed itself to my breasts. He knew that I had a big mouth to make up for the majority of the time when it was silenced by the drugs. He needed this job. He knew to look but not touch. The sight he had gorged on for five minutes went into his brain in the place marked 'Wank', filed for later use, when in his room in the nurses' home, he could 'bring the bitch down a peg or two' at his long and lonely leisure.

The beam flicked to the floor, lifted, then cast a cursory glance at the cot against the far wall, just to check the baby was still alive, just to check 'the bitch hadn't gone mad'. He withdrew and shut the door with a click.

CATH KILCOYNE (*b.* 1960)

Wrote at Drop-in Centre

Pleased to meet you
My name is Jesus
I can fly and do miracles

CHRISTINE DOHERTY

My Son

They tell me he
murdered a young girl
my son I love so much
moving to the country
to save him from
the corruption of
the city I worked
constantly to give
him a home and a
life free from harm
Now I spend my time
waiting for the train
to travel to the city
and visit the hospital

every week where he
will spend the
rest of his life.

MARY GUCKIAN (*b.* 1942)

Autumn was a moment away...

Autumn was a moment away
As my bike hurled towards
The open highway.

STEPHEN GARDNER (*b.* 1959)

I Don't Remember

I don't remember my thirty-seventh birthday
Nor my thirty-anything birthdays
But I can recall my 21st birthday vaguely
What a lot of cards came through the door
And what a lot of presents came to my hands.

And what a stash of money I got for the first time
£10 and £20 there, what a time I had counting it and
    counting it
I was like Prince Charles apart fae the lugs
What a time I had – you fair got carried away.

KEVIN ALLEN

Sky Over Bedlam

It dawned on me as we stared
up past roofs into walls climbing the sky
overlooking the significance of motorways
that we might all be drowning in the morning.

WENDY FRENCH

A Ward Round Postponed

Soon, I will say things I do not believe.
Soon. But it makes no difference. Since nothing
changes, nothing can change in the future.
I repeat this phrase over and over,
as I wait outside the ward round door,

and it feels uneasy, like a newsreel might,
inside a nineteen-thirties cinema
on the threshold of something never seen before.

I watched the documentary afternoon
emerge from the cinema in black and white.
I didn't think to ask what was showing;
it was not funny; no one was laughing.
The sunlight in the garden, where they went
to tear some strips of smoke, or perhaps dice
each other's heels, seemed to strafe the pavestones
as cloud passed like an aeroplane's wing.
Their legs were scissors in a cutting room
reflected in the patient-tended pond.
Soon, I thought, it will be different. It was.
The credits unrolled, the camera tracked
and people – doctors, social workers –
returned, taking their voices with themselves.

But I was not called. I did not appear where
the stacks of seats resembled gravestones piled
in the true image of the afternoon.
What they left behind was an old silence;
the reel stopped spinning and nothing had changed.

MARK JACOB (*b.* 1958)

Early Evening

Early evening here at last at least
I am alone, alone in the sun on the
grass sitting with my back supported
by a tree. A power mower chug chugs.
The gardener picks up sticks in the

patch where I sit, so I'll have to
move soon. I can't be still for more
than five minutes. The wind in the
leaves, almost silent, long shadows
creep closer as the sun sinks lower –
sunbathers converge in corners then
leave one by one until I am here alone
then I hear the wood pigeon and I hear
the blackbird and I hear a car, I hear
a door, I hear voices I hear footsteps
and another door slams, the gate creaks
then click click closes and still I am
here being still, a hero to myself un-
curling and curling my toes while seeds
float by almost invisible in the fading
light. I can't be still for more than
five minutes. (I can't be still for more
than five minutes.)

LARRY BUTLER (*b.* 1944)

Day Release

and the journey hard to believe –
each turn in the lanes
veering to home – yet so soon,

winter's sun fading, the afternoon
spent. And soon the nurses
are asking *Did you have*

a nice time; a nice
visit home? I didn't tell them
what the light was like

as I stepped under our lintel,
how in the kitchen our mewing tom in greeting
pressed furry warmth against my shaky legs. I keep

the dapple of these memories to hold against
the moment in our bedroom when I saw the imprint
of the separated person; the cold

hot-water bottle's rib
marking a rumple in the place where once
we had lain warm.

ANGELA MORTON (*b.* 1936)

A Musician's Wife

Between the visits to the shock ward
The doctors used to let you play
On the old upright Baldwin
Donated by a former patient
Who is said to be quite stable now.

And all day long you played Chopin,
Badly and hauntingly, when you weren't
Screaming on the porch that looked
Like an enormous birdcage. Or sat
In your room and stared out at the sky.

You never looked at me at all.
I used to walk down to where the bus stopped
Over the hill where the eucalyptus trees
Moved in the fog, and stared down
At the lights coming on, in the white rooms.

And always, when I came back to my sister's
I used to get out the records you made
The year before all your terrible trouble,
The records the critics praised and nobody bought
That are almost worn out now.

Now, sometimes I wake in the night
And hear the sound of dead leaves
Against the shutters. And then a distant
Music starts, a music out of an abyss,
And it is dawn before I sleep again.

WELDON KEES (1914–55)

The Man of Distinction

St Mary Abbots Hospital, Kensington, psychiatric wing

Where speechfolk with most disparate cries
addressed the loosest possible agenda,

or null with drugs, slumped over tables,
the horror backed behind the face,

one there was, silent was,
admitted to that company:

a man of distinction, it was whispered,
not in those words. A male nurse told me

he had the CBE. An elderly
number in loosest possible hospital issue

dressing gown, he veered with a cane
or sat appalled in the day room. He'd

no family, no clothes, no short-term
memory, he couldn't recall

as, the place to piss,
or anything much but his name he spoke

in the loosest possible manner of speaking,
a quailing proposition, rather than

fact, poor one. Pale breath, his face
was nonetheless indeed distinguished:

an eagle head upon a forsaken body
and soul, tipped, bladed nose

and ruined eyes like splintered flint
wondering what had brought him to this pass

or made these things to be.

Later I found out who he was
and the field of his distinction:

psychiatry.

KIT WRIGHT (*b.* 1944)

On the Run from Tooting Bec Hospital

Passed another litter bin
Poor pickings from tourist treasures.
Soup kitchen blues, Red Cross blanket
Wrapped around me
I sleep in the park, just another dosser.

MARTIN BROWNLEE (*b.* 1954)

The Volunteer

My father's had electricity shot through him
and nobody must know

Will he be blackened like lightning trees
lying sideways in the wetlands?
My huge horse-chestnut father
who'd made my special saddle on his bike
when I was little

'It was voluntary'
My mother whispered of sums
mumbled all night that never added up
of days hunched over the table
his hands ringed in two black tunnels
for his eyes to look through
and not see
'I was at my wits' end'

So this patient voluntary man crept home
with two rough circles at his temples
where they'd jump-started him.

'It's shingles,' my mother explained
as she hurried past the neighbours
My job was to take him by the hand
and unobtrusively
to lead him round the town
re-teach him all the names of all the streets
he'd always known, and how
to use his telephone
so his secretary wouldn't guess

He was not allowed out by himself

My father's had electricity shot through him
and nobody must know

JO PESTEL (*b.* 1942)

Poem for a Psychiatric Conference

'Thou thyself art the subject of my discourse.'
BURTON, preface to *The Anatomy of Melancholy*

'Melancholy is ... the character of mortality.'
BURTON, 'The First Partition'

I

When Marsyas the satyr played and lost
Against the god Apollo on the pipes,
The god lacked magnanimity. He skinned
The howling creature to his bones and tripes,
There in the nightmare canvas by Lorraine
Arcadia is green, and deaf to pain.

Perhaps the melancholy are unwise
To contemplate too closely this one death,
Since they may come to think that agony's
The consequence of merely drawing breath
And that the world itself is mad, to let
The mind inspect the facts it can't forget.

II

You were staring, one teatime, into the sink
When the voice made its awful suggestion. It seems
You were really, or ought to be, somebody else
In a different house, with a different wife –
May I speak plainly? the voice enquired.
It glozed, like the serpent in Milton –
Turned out for *years* you'd been making it up:
The kitchen, for one thing, the tiles and the draining-
    board,
Drawing-pinned postcards and lists of to-do's,
Even the crap round the back of the freezer.
The evidence *after all spoke for itself.*

The view up the steps to the garden, for instance,
The lawn with its slow-worm, the ruinous glasshouse
Up at the top, where the hurricane left it half-standing.
The woman next door as she pinned out her washing.
The weathercock's golden irregular wink
In the breeze from the sea to its twin on the spire
A mile off. Besides, the grey Channel itself
Setting out for the end of the world
Was the wrong stretch of water beside the wrong town.
You stood with your hands in your pockets and waited.
Very well, then, the God in the details disclosed:
Bus-tickets, receipts, phone numbers of people
You shouldn't have met in the pub
At the wrong time of day, the wrong year
With the wrong block of sunlight to stand
In the doorway. Your tread on the stair-carpet:
Wrong. Your skin between the freezing sheets
At dusk: an error. No matter the cause.
There is error, but not correspondingly cause.

III

The name of your case is *depression*
Although Doctor Birmingham favours
A failure of nerve. The files on the desk
In his office are fifty years old
And he, it seems, is just pretending
That he works here, sharing your gloom
And your startled gaze out at the slice
Of bitter-green grass where a bottle
Keeps rolling about in the wind
At the top of the city, where everything –
Buildings, the streetmap, the people –
Has run out of steam and delivered the ground
To an evil Victorian madhouse
Complete with cupola and coalhole
Which may or may not have shut down,
Though the bus shelter waits at the gate.

The overcooked smell is like weeping,
The cries are like nursery food
And the liverish paint on the wailing walls
Is a blatant incitement to stop being good.
Call for Nurse Bromsgrove and Sir Stafford
Wolverhampton, call Rugeley the Porter.
There are vast misunderstandings
Lurking in the syntax by the stairs.

The worst of it is, there are rooms
Not far off, waiting and book-filled
For someone like you to arrive and possess them;
A hedge at the window, and lilacs, and past them
A street that can take a whole morning
To saunter downhill past the flint walls and ginnels
Adding up to harmless privacy. This perhaps
Is what some of the mad people contemplate,
Reading their hands on a bench in the park
In their ill-fitting clothes, as if someone must come
To explain and restore and say *Put that behind you.*

SEAN O'BRIEN (*b.* 1952)

Leaving Hospital

Five months inside
the shell of a Work-House/Asylum:
sixty years to paint over
the smell of cruelty and innocent faces
they jammed between the bricks.

I want to be an undercoat for a little longer
and tell dirty jokes to the nineteenth
century.

They're forcing me out
into Now.
Into an upside-down,
inside-out Gulliver's world.

Where everything's changed:
the streets, the cafés, the toilets.

PETER STREET (*b*. 1948)

After the Silence

The moon stood
Like a drunk
Looking up the street
Wondering,

Is this the street,
Is this the town,
What happened,
And who did I meet?

Oh there were happier times,
There's no denying the fact,
But they're over.
It's done. That's that.

DERMOT HEALY (*b*. 1947)

The New Town

The first days I went to town
I used to pass them;
In time found out they were
The hospital, the asylum.

From the beginning I had
An affinity for both.
The General I walked to from Glencar,
St Columba's from The Point.

In one my hand was put in plaster,
In the other I was given librium.
A couple of years I spent
Cocooned in delirium,

Till language like a nurse
Pitched her tent without a sound.
Enough light here to write by,
Enough remorse to put it down.

But my mind didn't flower.
The break refused to set.
My hand will never make a fist,
And you haunt me yet.

DERMOT HEALY

Blacker than Before

for Sylvia Tang

Black windows, black doors, black oil out of black floors
Slippery black like a blackbird's wing
I can feel him inside me,
I can feel him beneath me
Taste the black oblivion of his wet face
Taste him sticky limbed – under me in red lace
The black makes the yellow-blue bright
While the red and black bleed into a dark thrashing –
Blacker than before
Keeping me away from me and myself.

And from my fingertips black tar weeps into a black sky
Of a terminal black night gifting me with a fine stark
    vision
A vision clear and light and black as can only be my black
    night
I told the doctor so but she could not, did not know
That this is me now – in love, enraptured
With the blackest sex of the highest lands, of other spaces,
The black birthing from my perfect hands, from spaces
    gone,
Keeping me, keeping me away from the voices – black
Blacker than before
Keeping me away from me and myself.

CLAIRE BAYARD-WHITE (*b.* 1954)

The Sound of My Head

After 'Il Bambino Malato', a child's
head in beeswax by Medardo Rosso

On my birthday I come in from hiding
in the cold sand under the house
where I've been talking to my friends, the lizards.
Pale sand caked on switch-welts is my new set of ribs.
She says now I'm four, stop crying.

I taste somebody's piss like pennies
on my lemon-coloured birthday cake
and I pretend not to know I'm their animal.
They weigh each feather in my head again,
set some alight, some adrift.

I want to cry with a fish hawk's voice
that's the same sound as the sky tearing.
If I'm quiet as a cricket in a brush fire
they'll laugh at their little birthday joke.
Or she'll break my face for talking crazy.

Maybe I was born crazy, gone fizzy in the head
like a melon left too long in the sun.
That's what they say, doing those things that hurt.
I think of the little toenails on my dried rabbit's-foot
and decide to bury it in the morning.

When I retch on my mother's deep-throat kiss
she says the brown bitter stuff in my ears
is the turds of scorpions that nest in my head while
   I sleep.
They sting my brain to make mad dreams
and if I wake them at night I'll die.

She yells I'm more stupid every day,
asks can I feel my brain shrinking?
Sometimes I stand off to one side,
shake my head, scared to hear a rattle.

SCOTT VERNER (*b.* 1929)

Her Large Smile

*After 'La Grande Rieuse', the plaster
head of a woman by Medardo Rosso*

Coming so soon after the stomach pump
my sister's radiance
is like a sequined sheet in a morgue.

Like the sun caught in a rain puddle
her smile's too big for her face.
Her eyes, still trying to find their way home,
bond with mine in a flash of acetylene.

Bothered by a breeze or distant voices,
she shatters like a thermometer.
Out of sharp splinters her rage
runs off in all directions.

I can't build a rapport with lightning
but I want to help her, remind her
I'm as close to her shivers as she is –
tremors from childhood quakes:
when someone said 'smile' she flinched,
'sit in my lap' and she wailed.

She announces plans for a famous career –
gathering spider webs deep in the pine woods
which she'll carry home intact

in her miraculous hands,
then melt them gently
to replenish the tears of lost children.

Unaware of the weight of her silent mouth
she hits me head-on with a large smile
that bruises the back of my eyes.
I'm scared what might happen after sundown.

SCOTT VERNER

The Sick Image of My Father Fades

The sick image of my father fades.
When I was three he used to take me
Tied up in a sack to the cliff's edge
And threaten to throw me over. The wind
Was ghastly, and his hands shook with terror.
I whimpered like a fretful dog. Fear
Stole over me, and I shrieked and screamed.

My father said, shall I break your legs
Before throwing you over? You should then land
On the sand without the sudden crunch crunch
Of breaking bones. I looked up at him, pleading.
Then he would laugh out loud like a normal man,
And let me clamber back onto his back, so that I forgot
The sheer drop from the cliff's edge, just for a moment.

JOHN HORDER (*b.* 1936)

The Cradle

I still remember my shivering birthday,
a hand crafted suitcase was my cradle.
I was wrapped in cream-coloured consciousness,
nagging hopes in something better,
deserved only by people with clean hands.

I had many toys: a wooden cross, the abacus,
pots and pans, pins and needles, punch and judy,
a gravestone, an ivory tower in which Barbie lived,
(unreliable and beautiful with a disjointed arm),
a piece of broken glass (sparkled in the sunlight),
black and white photos of unknown relatives
and of course the rosary; the endless rosary.

This I shared with my speechless brothers and sisters,
who were almost happy about what they did not have.
I grew up slowly, restricted, not trusting I was alive.
Myths and legends were obdurate teachers, shadows
        enemies.
I knew one day I would escape.
I ran and ran to the edge of the horizon and beyond.

The island where I landed was bewildering,
soundless sleep overcame me, deep, long, wide.
I awoke with a little, leather suitcase,
it had followed me without wings, without feet.
Inside, among the familiar estrangements,
I faced for the first time my own melted memories.

VALERIA MELCHIORETTO (*b.* 1967)

Survivor

I went back to lay the dark ghosts of my childhood,
but standing in the garden of my first home
I could find none – only
the tranquillity of autumn air.
The house was smaller than I remembered
not dark-pervaded or menacing,
just ordinary and smiling in the sun.

Faint memories seeped from the upstairs window,
but they were of domesticity
and hide-and-seek rather than fear or pain.
It was so different from what I'd remembered
– my childhood ghosts were not the house's fault.

As I turned to leave, I saw a beech tree growing
on one side of the garden,
and remembered planting a single branch there one week
before I left the house. Against all odds it had flowered
into maturity. Like me, it had survived.
So now when I think of my first home,
instead of dark ghosts, I remember the beech tree.

MALA MASON (*b.* 1946)

Eisriesenwelt

*Eisriesenwelt – the Ice Giants' World – is the largest ice cave
in the world, high in the Austrian Alps. It is full of ice formations
such as the Icewall and the Icedoor.*

In the world of the ice giants
I'm not afraid.

Today, I glided into the cave.
I wore glass shoes.

When I held my hand
against the light

I could see the veins
tunnelling through my palm

like a system of caves.
I stripped,

so the ice could fill me.

*

When I left home
I sculpted my parents in ice
but they kept melting.
The tutors complained.
They said water was formless.
I needed a fridge large as Eisriesenwelt,
26 miles long, to store my art.

So I tried glass.
Sometimes I touch the ice
and think it's fire –
the white heat of the kiln
where glass sculptures are cast.

I tried to rebuild my grandmother's greenhouse.
I made glass trees, glass rain, and a glass grandmother,

but they annealed too fast. They cracked.

*

Welcome to my studio
full of figures and towers.
Some of the towers are people.

Some of the people are towers.
Don't blame the artist.
I make what the ice-giants dictate.
If they say *stay in the studio overnight,*
I stay.

They made me carve
a stone dress for my mother.
I am not to blame
for its weight.

I was the lacemaker
who used frost
instead of silk
for her underclothes.

*

I created an entire wardrobe –

a dress of green ice
for my mother the sea,

a dress of blue ice
for my mother the sky,

a dress of black ice
for my mother the earth.

Her body shone through the green dress
like a reef.

Her body shone through the blue dress
like the sun.

Her body shone through the black dress
like a corpse.

My hands were raw from sewing
molten gossamers of spun glass
which shattered
when worn.

She was a tower of broken windows.

 *

My mother has put all her clothes on,
armouring herself against me.
If I ask the right question
one of the dresses will answer.
They speak different languages.
There is the language of glass –
window-glass and lead-crystal,
and the language of ice –
blue, green and black ice.

She leads me to a house
where I spend five years
surrounded by emerald and ruby tears,
by turquoise and sapphire tears.
She has shed so many jewels
they form seas in our rooms.
I call my mother's seas
Sea of Sadness, the Bitter Sea,
Sea of Madness, the Guilty Sea.

 *

Welcome to our sitting-room.
It's hard to cross it, so we don't.

We're those two
facing each other across the ice.

The walls are furred.
My mother is waiting for me to defrost them.

Long blue icicles hang from the ceiling
like rain from a permanent storm.

Even in caves, the wind can blow out light.
The draught has plunged us into darkness.

My mother's tears freeze. They fall
onto her body like stitches in a glass dress

knitted from the seas of her sadness.
Dresses within dresses. Mothers within daughters.

Because I am young. Because I am alive,
the Icedoor is open. I remember

we passed it before the fridge took over.
Perhaps on a postcard, in a letter.

It was a mouth. My mouth.
I said yes. I'll visit. Every weekend.

Yes. I'll come back, defrosting,
cleaning the scraps from the shelves.

Mow the lawn. Mow the mountains of Austria.

I got up. I slipped. I crawled along the floor.
Down frozen waterfalls I slid. Down the Icewall.

The cable-car was waiting for me.

The inn was warm. My life was warm.

PASCALE PETIT (*b.* 1953)

What You Need

This is what you need
if you're found face down in the snow
or floating underwater
with an arrow through your foot:
Two layers of ivory keys of the cembalo
a splash of notes from the kids in the corner
the wisdom of ancient Mexican potions
the shine of a gold-leafed harpsichord
black notes from the beak of a falcon
and a pile of tidy stones
to show you where you are.

LUCY COLLARD (*b.* 1956)

The Butterfly

He was a butterfly
And he had all
The words on his wings,
And he said to the moth
'I love the light,
And I know how it burns.'

DES MCHALE (1958–96)

Calling Back the Body

(with extracts from a relaxation tape)

The sweat-shop starts early, sewing machines
clattering over abstracted skin;
closer, pins and needles in the back of my hand

I am calling back the body:
find a comfortable place to sit or lie.

It takes off whenever it's troubled,
respond to nothing for a while
on walkabout, at the edge and beyond
of skin. I lie awake wondering
about the etiquette of summoning the thing,
as if it were an elevator of lacy wrought iron.
Which floor for witchcraft?
At this hour, it has the benefit of my doubt,
I will name the dirty stop-out, hexed and sexed he.

I am calling back the body from his desert island.
Still, no postcard
and too much seagull noise on the line.
We were discussing prescriptions
before he went a*nd you may want to feel
the damp sand beneath your feet
a deep rosy colour... it's late in the day.*
His time, not mine. And I need him here
for a serious talk, ... intense, pointed,
the sort when *feeling flows like honey*
through the jaw muscles.

'Oh you whooooo', I am calling back
the body, pouring him into childish limbs.
He is when I was young and mother's
siren song persuaded me out of sleep.

BRUCE BARNES (*b.* 1948)

Smile

When at long last the daystar burns blue
and the sun splits the ice – I'm ready.
To splash hot kisses on the face
of every man, woman, Jack in the bus.
To bamboozle their sleepy senses
with lewd lyrics set to a tune
that everyone knew, but until that
very second thought happily forgotten.
To love with violence and with patronage,
spew laughter, refreshing as warm spindrift,
over god's winter-worn out,
desperate-for-fags, woolly-hatted,
half-hibernating creatures.
I sit hard down on my excitement –
wipe a way through the smeared window.
Mankind snores or attends to its ears
as two collarless dogs embrace.
I smile. My first smile of the year –
the size and shine of a partial eclipse.
On a morning like this, when at long last

V.G. LEE (*b.* 1949)

Paquida

The young black girl's face
hardly visible on my dark porch
late last night
I asked her in.
Paquida is seventeen,
lives in the Shelter.

She came here
with her father a year ago.
He died in April.
The first person I've met

from Mississippi State, tho I learnt
to spell it when I was eight.

She stands to leave searching
for the words she wants –
'I been drinking' she says
'but A'm still myself.'

Gust of a thousand winds
blew through me,
shut the dimming stars,
gathered in the soft-black
folds of her full skirt.
Ghost of a dream at dawn.

I think of myself
at that age
leaving my parents' house,
nothing could reach me
sad to the point of death.
How could I survive?

LOUISE C. CALLAGHAN (*b.* 1948)

Sign Writing

The sign, and the way it relates us to death,
to separation, to otherness.

I

Pre-dawn I am voluble
Air's charged with incipient grey
A trail of ash on the earth
It is patched with light again
Tattered sentences
Suffused with its energy
In the sky
The incised letters blaze

2

Now wind turns a page of the garden
Each sign speaks for itself
Opens the mouth of its own stilled vacancy
Studded with all the names
Of its carpet of growth, then walks away
Into silence. The trees
Shoot up again, blocks of
Houses in mist.
You stretch in front of a mirror
Your nightdress beside the opened novel

3

Large areas have been removed
In a project called 'replacing the sky'
And did you know which birds
Are omens at large in the sky's page
Wings finger the scales of the air
Finding the thermals, the steep upward draught

All the signs cry out for the key
Later, for me and for you
These stanzas, stances

JOHN WELCH (*b.* 1942)

from Canto CXV

The scientists are in terror
             and the European mind stops
Wyndham Lewis chose blindness
             rather than have his mind stop.
Night under wind mid garofani,
             the petals are almost still
Mozart, Linnaeus, Sulmona,
When one's friends hate each other
             how can there be peace in the world?
Their asperities diverted me in my green time.
A blown husk that is finished
             but the light sings eternal
a pale flare over marshes
             where the salt hay whispers to tide's change
Time, space,
             neither life nor death is the answer.
And of man seeking good,
             doing evil.
In meiner Heimat
             where the dead walked
                          and the living were made of cardboard.

EZRA POUND (1885–1972)

A Common Cause

Dear boy, uncommon brother, fourth apostle
My next of kin, you helped me yesterday
Among retreating dreams and childhood daisies
We briefly held the wicked world at bay.
Today within the grounds of my asylum
I can mouth anew the words we used to say.
There are tigers at the bottom of our bed
Still they threaten: Matthew, Mark and Luke and John
Well then, let me chant a rhyme or two to rid us
Say a prayer to ward them off and then move on.

We can do without the suffering of sinners
We can do without the dark satanic mills
We can do without the cheeky little devils
We can do without the funny elfin dells
We can do without the curly locks and moonshine
We can do without Walt Disney wishing wells
We can do without the messages from Heaven
We can do without Grimm's tales and fairy bells.

From Hell, Hull and Halifax,
good Lord deliver us.

Noli me tangere.

SUSAN GAUKROGER (*b.* 1943)

Mah Towing

She go to Mato every day
She go with plastic mice.
She mato to the chimney fire
She say to Mato, 'Nice!'

And then with Mato underground,
To Mato she say, 'Creep!'
Her stocking is to Mato sexy
Made to Mato's sleep.

Her perfume get Tomato mad
She run to Mato fair,
She play with knife, she take her life
To Mato's everywhere.

To Mato's tomb she taking me
I feel he is a fake.
In time to Mato breakfast come
To Mato, wide awake!

So now to Mato she say, 'Hey!'
'I think I need some more.'
To Morrow he stay next to her,
Of that you can be sure.

GARY ERNEST KAY (*b.* 1960)

The Kitchen Chair

Think of the kitchen chair,
Then having thought,
Write down what you have thought.
Then having written down what you have thought
Think about the kitchen chair again.
Then having thought about it
Long enough
Ask yourself this question:
Has the kitchen chair changed
In your mind
Since you have written about it?
Read what you have written,
Then sit back and think
And having thought,
Write it all down.
This will keep you ungainfully occupied
For the rest of your working life.
They will point you out at Compendium:
'There goes the man who writes the kitchen chair poems.
Everybody thinks he is the new Maya Kovsky;
If you want my privatized opinion
I am sick and tired of his kitchen chairs –
Kitchen chairs this, kitchen chairs that,
Are there no other chairs in the world?
Chairs of this and Chairs of that, Boardroom chairs,
Chairs of Grants and non-Grants,
Chairs bolted down at the DSS – he'll soon find out
And anyway if he wants to make a living out of writing
There is more money in bedroom chairs.'
Having heard all that, think again, write it all down.
Await no payment, no thanks, no fob watch of olden times.
Clear off and get out of the kitchen.

JOHN RETY (*b.* 1930)

Mr Tosun

Mr Tosun takes out his
measuring tape to
measure the world.
From home and to where he is
is a good distance.
He measures so precisely,
methodically sixty metres
and or thereabouts from the
end of the world to where
Mr Tosun looking sharp lives.

He pooh poohs all notion
that he might be wrong.
'I'm never wrong.'
And there he is in blue
looking at the clouds,
his measurements so exact.

I know Mr Tosun only slightly
for he doesn't mix with people.
He prefers his own exalted company.
And as he splashes on the sea front,
little children throw stones at his
greying head but he is never ridiculed
by grownups. For grownups he is
a scientist and a man of vision.

Mr Tosun has farted. He is measuring his
fart and the drop in the ocean of a pebble.
Dear Mr Tosun is always busy.
For he has a lot to do.

FATMA DURMUSH (*b.* 1959)

The Grand Old Duke of York

The Grand Old Duke of York
Well he had quite an army
Ten thousand soldiers in his command
And every one of them thought he was barmy.

Every morning after breakfast time
When each man had had his fill
The Duke would lead them from the castle grounds
And march them up a hill.

Then when they'd got to the top of the hill
Whether in sunshine or in rain
The Duke would simply turn them round
And march them down again.

At the top of the hill they knew where they were
At the bottom they knew where they'd been
But when they were only halfway up
Confusion always seemed to set in.

To this very day the hill still exists
And halfway up is a picnic sight
Well the sign at the bottom says: '*Halfway up*'
But I'm not sure if it is right.

'Cos if you climb the hill right to the top
(And this would make the Old Duke frown)
There's another sign which appears to say:
'Picnic Area – *Halfway Down.*'

KEITH THORNLEY

Night at the Blind Beggar

Easy-peasy they said, a simple job,
money for old rope. Here's a drink.
Go to the Blind Beggar in Whitechapel
between this hour and this hour.

Sink a slow thoughtful pint or two,
a tough young bucko in his suit and tie,
out for the evening on a mission,
the bystander with the job of seeing nothing.

A quiet night, the light fading, traffic
on the High Street, music on the jukebox.
Then at 8.30 Ronnie walks in with a Mauser
and blows a man's head all over the room.

Hadn't bargained for that.
Not that sort of drink.
Our man sees everything and nothing.
That's it he's out of there.

Jumped the District Line, at Paddington
the first train anywhere took him west
into an ordinary life: job, mortgage,
wife, kids, the years becoming more years.

Except the long days and longer nights
of all the rest of him are spattered
by the bits of brain on the wall
and blood over his white shirtfront.

This is his tale of how he got lost.
Dogget he says into the strange silence
he inhabits, the question mark as ever
slung around his shoulder. *Dog ate my dinner.*

KEN SMITH (*b.* 1938)

'Loss of Recent Memory'

A gentleman,
He waits to be introduced, shakes our hands,
Takes our coats, pours out the sherry, then stands

Watching faces.
He has blue eyes, smooth white hair, a white skin.
He stoops forward to listen. We begin

Small-talk, chit-chat:
What we do, where we live, our holidays.
He lives nearby, he thinks. He thinks he stays

By the seaside
In a hotel or flat; perhaps with friends.
Children join us. His conversation ends.

It's supper-time.
We eat and talk in a scarlet sunset.
He says he comes from Hindhead, can't forget

The years spent there,
His work, his home, his wife. Now he's retired,
He thinks. Off sick, he thinks. Have we admired

The bowl of plums?
He touches the bloom with his finger-tips,
Gently touches and strokes his cheeks and lips.

Fruit, cheese, coffee.
He clears plates, passes cups, fetches ashtrays,
Draws the curtains, fondles the dog, his gaze

Always on us,
Doubting, questioning. I feel like a sum
Too hard to add up; or a conundrum

Without answer.
It's late, we must go. He brings coats, a light
To guide us down the drive. We say good-night.

RUTH SILCOCK (*b.* 1926)

And Why Not??

I want to change my name
Not for purposes of disguise you understand
Or running away, though there's a thought
I just want, well, more music, every day
And when I met 'Mr Orazio Rea'
Desire came and grew and a certain discontent
With my own long-known name
So I thought, what a choice, from so many
Shall I go for something new but low key?
Pomegranate has class, crisp, a little tart
Or Banana, what new strength lies there
I can leave Literature alone in the main
Though I do have my Scarlett days and
Can stamp my feet with the best of them
It'll mean a little work for the bureaucrats

But who cares? I shall sign 'Anaglypta' if I wish
Or Marmalade is cosy, Fahrenheit would cause a stir
I might choose Sphere when feeling under-confident
Or Lapis Lazuli, when I'm blue
And you can always trust a Burnt Umber
Or maybe something startling like Queue
I'd need caution with Volkswagen or Volvo
For fear I might be swiftly overlooked
But Lagonda has a certain sultry something
And I could hide the new bus pass in the plush
So I'm open to suggestions on a Wednesday
From any interested party or a peer
But there has to be some sense of it belonging
This name will last, I hope, for many a year
We don't want those bureaucrats too dizzy
And I need, naturally, to recognize what's mine
So I'll keep myself tuned in to all the music
Of any likely word I might just hear
For now I have decided not to tarry
The changing of my name is very near

JOSIE KILDEA (*b.* 1937)

Dilemma

He played my silken button
And he tugged my tousled hair
His passion loosed he bit my neck
But didn't really care.

He touched my heart with kindness
And loved me warm and tender
He kissed my wounds and held my hand
But overlooked my gender.

What can I do to find a blend
It seems to be my luck
To find the bastards sexy
Whereas gentlemen don't fuck.

W.L. (*b.* 1954)

At The Braque Exhibition

I heard colour sing today and
You were the missing flute
So necessary for the full orchestra
You'd have loved the paintings
Rich chrome yellow in the centre
With purple, olive and sage green
Planes of coral, cream and grey
There's nothing so intoxicating
As colour, its warp and weft
Making shadows from solids
Objects into shadows
You'd have liked the artist's frugality
Rarely leaving his home
Looking and looking more at the same thing,
The discoveries of a lifetime in one studio
The big bird alighting on the canvas
Albatrossing white or black across the space
Above the intricate map of a cubist view
It made me think of your absence
The time we lost when you were gone
Just the once you said, after years of being cured,
'They took away my colours,' and afresh I understood
At the concert of colour today
When I got drunk on Braque

JOSIE KILDEA (*b.* 1937)

On a Portrait of William Blake
by Francis Bacon

His neck is an upturned anvil
Supporting the peeled boulder of his head.
Flesh, pink and grey-blue, washed
Over with nerve-ends like infant sea-worms.
Primitive responses – touched and recoiled
Form in a bruising that cuts through
Self-awareness to pure pain, pure
Reaction. As if he evolved from a spine
And the telephone-cables of nerves were flushed
Through with blue or yellow dye, exposed
Ganglions and broken fuse-ends, and
The evolution ended there. A museum-piece.
A machine-cleaned carcass flailing
At the suggestion of a touch.

Around him there is black night, his neck
Disappears, merges with it,
Emerges from it with eyes closed,
Great ears drawn to earth by lobes of lead.
The puttied gash of mouth sinks
Down to two pink thumbprints at each edge.
So naked: oniony silver skin swelling
To trowelled-on grout around his shoulders,
Beams of bones protruding through. Any
Probing would induce a trauma.

This head has watched while something bled it white.
Now its eyes are closed behind cuttlefish lids.

PAUL CLARK (*b.* 1969)

Clare Leaves High Beach

for Steve and Sheila

Others also were muttering and went
Each alone on the designated ways
Tipping their headgear. Said Doctor Allen,
His kind keeper, for such men
The best company in the world is trees.

Turmoil in the head, tempest: a beech
With its arms ripped off, the yellow bone
Showing, rags everywhere, the shriek
Of roots in air, and the mind reached
Into the crippling. He bolted then, for home.

Lay down, beat, his head the needle
North for the morning, he lay between
His two wives quietly and the love was equalled.
Woke. They were gone. The sadness welled
Out of the ground and through his eyes again.

A face came over him, it had a crown
That bulged from a wreath of hair, a face
As large and a dome as bald as the moon
Beamed down at him. It was his own:
Good-natured, cheerful, and quite crazed.

He lay for the north. Out of him travelled,
As though he bled, the love of certain trees
In place, a spire, a stile, a golden field,
Lapwing in thousands. How much he held
And must crawl after now on hands and knees!

DAVID CONSTANTINE (*b.* 1944)

Death of a Son

(who died in a mental hospital aged one)

Something has ceased to come along with me.
Something like a person: something very like one.
And there was no nobility in it
Or anything like that.

Something was there like a one year
Old house, dumb as stone. While the near buildings
Sang like birds and laughed
Understanding the pact

They were to have with silence. But he
Neither sang, nor laughed. He did not bless silence
Like bread, with words.
He did not forsake silence.

But rather, like a house in mourning
Kept the eye turned in to watch the silence while
The other houses like birds
Sang around him.
And the breathing silence neither
Moved nor was still.

I have seen stones: I have seen brick
But this house was made up of neither bricks nor stone
But a house of flesh and blood
With flesh of stone

And bricks for blood. A house
Of stones and blood in breathing silence with the other
Birds singing crazy on its chimneys.
But this was silence,

This was something else, this was
Hearing and speaking though he was a house drawn
    Into silence, this was
        Something religious in his silence,

    Something shining in his quiet,
This was different this was altogether something else:
    Though he never spoke, this
        Was something to do with death.

    And then slowly the eye stopped looking
Inward. The silence rose and became still.
The look turned to the outer place and stopped,
    With the birds still shrilling around him.
        And as if he could speak

He turned over on his side with his one year
Red as a wound
He turned over as if he could be sorry for this
And out of his eyes two great tears rolled, like stones,
    and he died.

JON SILKIN (*b.* 1930)

In back of the real

railroad yard in San José
    I wandered desolate
in front of a tank factory
    and sat on a bench
near the switchman's shack.

A flower lay on the hay on
    the asphalt highway
– the dread hay flower
    I thought – It had a
brittle black stem and
    corolla of yellowish dirty
spikes like Jesus' inchlong
    crown, and a soiled
dry center cotton tuft
    like a used shaving brush
that's been lying under
    the garage for a year.

Yellow, yellow flower, and
    flower of industry,
tough spikey ugly flower,
    flower nonetheless,
with the form of the great yellow
    Rose in your brain!
This is the flower of the World.

ALLEN GINSBERG (1926–97)

Half-an-Hour

to Meraud Guevara

... and grass grows round the door. The ground,
Without, is grained with root and stone
And yellow-stained where sunlight pours on sand
Through listlessly stirred chestnut-leaves.
This is the long-sought still retreat,
This is the house, the quiet land,
My spirit craves.

        A burning sound,
Uninterrupted as the flow of high-noon's light
Down on the trees from whence it emanates,
The song of the cigales, slowly dissolves
All other thought than that of absolute
Consent, even to anxious transience.

Aix-en-Provence

DAVID GASCOYNE (*b.* 1916)

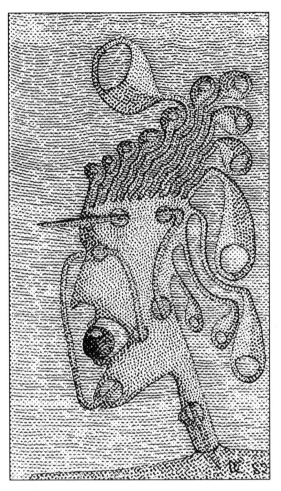

Thoughts, 1982. David Chick (b. 1947)

ACKNOWLEDGEMENTS

The publishers are grateful to the authors, their representatives and publishers for permission to reproduce copyright material in this anthology as follows:

KEVIN ALLEN: 'I Don't Remember' copyright © Kevin Allen 1997, by permission of the author; JOE ASSER: 'Arriving Early' and 'Don't Flinch' copyright © Joe Asser 1997, by permission of the author; JILL BAMBER: 'The Shadow-Board' copyright © Jill Bamber 1997, by permission of the author; BRUCE BARNES: 'Calling Back the Body' copyright © 1997 by Bruce Barnes, by permission of the author; ELIZABETH BARTLETT: 'The Visitors' copyright © Elizabeth Bartlett 1979, from *A Lifetime of Dying* (1979), by permission of Harry Chambers/Peterloo Poets; CAROL BATTON: 'Not a Buttercup' copyright © Carol Batton 1997, by permission of the author; CLAIRE BAYARD-WHITE: 'Blacker than Before' copyright © Claire Bayard-White 1997, by permission of the author; JOHN BERRYMAN: 'The Song of the Demented Priest' from *Collected Poems: 1937–1971* (Farrar, Straus & Giroux, New York, 1971), by permission of Farrar, Straus & Giroux, Inc. and Faber and Faber: copyright © Kate Donahue Berryman 1989; THOMAS BLACKBURN: 'Hospital for Defectives' copyright © Thomas Blackburn 1958, from *The Next World* (Putnam, London, 1958), by permission of Julia Blackburn; JEAN 'BINTA' BREEZE: 'Riddym Ravings' from *Spring Cleaning* (Virago, London, 1992) copyright © Jean 'Binta' Breeze 1992, by permission of Little Brown and 57 Productions, London; MARTIN BROWNLEE: 'On the Run from Tooting Bec Hospital' copyright © Martin Brownlee 1997, by permission of the author; LARRY BUTLER: 'Early Evening' copyright © Larry Butler 1997, by permission of the author; LOUISE C. CALLAGHAN: 'Paquida' copyright © Louise C. Callaghan 1997, by permission of the author; NORMAN CAMERON: excerpt from his translation of 'Ravings II' from Arthur Rimbaud, *A Season in Hell* (Anvil Press, London, 1994) copyright © Jane Aiken Hodge 1994, by permission of Anvil Press; IAIN CRICHTON SMITH: 'Sea' copyright © Iain Crichton Smith 1997, by permission of the author; PAUL CLARK: 'On a Portrait of William Blake by Francis Bacon' copyright © Paul Clark 1997, by permission of the author; ROBERT COLE: 'From One Helpstone Man to Another' copyright © Robert Cole 1997, first published in *Ambit*, by permission of the author; LUCY COLLARD: 'What You Need' copyright © Lucy Collard 1997, by permission of the author; DAVID CONSTANTINE: 'Clare Leaves High Beach' from *Selected Poems* (Bloodaxe Books, Newcastle, 1991) copyright © David Constantine 1991, by permission of Bloodaxe Books; KAREN DAVIES: 'ha ha' copyright © Karen Davies 1988, by permission of the author; CHRISTINE DOHERTY: 'Wrote at the Drop-in Centre' copyright © Christine Doherty 1997, by permission of the author; IAN DUHIG: 'Clare's Jig #43' copyright © Ian Duhig 1997, by permission of the author; PAUL DURCAN: 'The Turkish Carpet' and 'Madman' copyright © Paul Durcan 1976 and 1985, from *A Snail in My Prime: New and Selected Poems* (1993), by permission of the Harvill Press; FATMA DURMUSH: 'In the Ocean' and 'Mr Tosun' copyright © Fatma Durmush 1997, by permission of the author; NICOLA EAST: 'To Sleep Perchance to Dream' copyright © Nicola East 1997, by permission of the author; T.S. ELIOT: 'Hysteria' copyright © Valerie Eliot 1969, from *Collected Poems 1909–1962* (by permission of Faber and Faber, London; HARRY FAINLIGHT: 'The Leaf' copyright © Ruth Fainlight 1986, from *Selected Poems* by Harry Fainlight, edited and introduced by Ruth Fainlight (Turret Books, London, 1986), by permission of Ruth Fainlight; WENDY FRENCH: 'Sky over Bedlam' copyright ©

INDEX OF AUTHORS

Translators are marked with an asterisk

THE CHARITIES

THE MENTAL HEALTH FOUNDATION is concerned with all aspects of mental health including both mental illness and learning disabilities. It plays a vital role in pioneering new approaches to prevention, treatment and care. The Foundation's work includes: allocating grants for research and community projects; contributing to the public debate; educating policy makers and health care professionals and striving to reduce the stigma attached to mental illness and learning disabilities. It depends upon voluntary donations from individuals, companies and trusts to carry out its activities.

MIND is the leading mental health charity in England and Wales. It works for a better life for people diagnosed, labelled or treated as mentally ill and campaigns for their right to lead an active and valued life in the community. Drawing on the knowledge and skills both of people who provide and use the mental health services, Mind has established itself not only as the largest independent provider of good quality care in the community, but also as an influential commentator on government policy in all areas of mental health.

SURVIVORS' POETRY is a national literature organization, founded in 1991, providing poetry workshops, readings, performances, publishing, outreach and training. Funded by the Arts Council of England, London Arts Board and several charitable trusts, it has created a national network of fourteen regional Survivors' Poetry groups with plans for a further twenty by 2001. Survivors' Poetry organizations are managed by mental health system survivors and disabled people, enabling the creative voice of survivors to gain strength, reaching the wider community to help dispel fear and prejudice.

❖ ❖ ❖

THE BETHLEM & MAUDSLEY NATIONAL BENEFIT POETRY PROJECT is working in collaboration with the Bethlem & Maudsley (NHS) Trust to use the 750th anniversary of the Royal Bethlem Hospital, Europe's oldest mental health institution, to raise money for the above charities, and to promote a more positive, informed and compassionate understanding of mental illness.